NICK ROBINS

ISBN: 1 871947 31 6
Published by

12 M… …les, SA68 0SA
…4484

CONTENTS

INTRODUCTION

The development and economy of our islands has been and will continue to be influenced by our ability to transport people, vehicles and goods across the sea. As an interested bystander (a professional geologist with my feet firmly ashore) I have watched the evolution of the ferry over the last three decades, and given my own professional experience I knew that I could write this story well; once I started, the book flowed easily.

There are many people who have helped in my endeavour, not least Miles Cowsill and John Hendy, but also a young, all demanding family who competed for my attention, as well as my father George who cast the first critical eye over the manuscript. The greatest help of all came from the previous writers, journalists and archivists who had taken the time to preserve, document and record over the years, the products of the naval architects and the shipbuilders, the triumphs and the disasters, and of course the seafarers and the passengers who are this story.

Of the many hours spent standing on windswept quays peering forlornly into the dusk in anticipation of the arrival of a particular favourite, one story above all others comes to mind. The *Claymore* was responsible for the Oban to Coll and Tiree service during the mid-1980s; leaving Oban at 0700 hours, passengers and their cars were allowed to board the previous evening depending on the availability of the six passenger cabins.

One frosty November night I parked my car on the car deck, went ashore for a couple of pints then turned in for the night. Sleep well? Not exactly, what with the intermittent growl of the bilge pump in an otherwise silent ship, and the violent scraping and banging coming from the car deck above, sleep was not part of the deal. Inspection the following morning revealed a very large and fierce looking ram tethered at the forward end of the car deck, a ram that was clearly excited at the prospect of meeting new ladyfolk on the islands.

I hope that you enjoy reading this book as much as I have enjoyed writing it.

Nick Robins
Crowmarsh
September 1995

FOREWORD

by CAPTAIN T V KINLEY

The development of the British 'vehicle' ferry is largely a phenomenon of the second half of the twentieth century. The very name 'vehicle' ferry provides a clue as to why this should be, for it was during this same period that the car population multiplied many times over. The British motorist and family soon developed the habit of going abroad with the car, not only to Ireland and the offshore islands but to all parts of the continent, thus creating a demand for shipping space that could not be met by conventional vessels, particularly during the summer. The result was the arrival of the car ferry on the short sea routes around our coasts. They came in all shapes and sizes, some had doors at the bow and stern, others at the stern only and in a few specialised ships, side doors, but the concept was so successful in developing new business for their owners that it was only a matter of time before they replaced virtually all existing ferries and became accepted as the only type of vessel for the short sea routes.

In due course the term "Car Ferry" became something of a misnomer for as vessels were replaced by larger ones they were able to carry coaches and every type of commercial vehicle.

I feel privileged to be part of this continuing revolution which now appears to be leaning towards high speed ferries. The full story is revealed in Nick Robin's fascinating book and I wish him every success.

The ***Pride of Dover*** and ***Pride of Calais*** *(FotoFlite)*

CHAPTER 1

THE EARLY ESTUARINE FERRIES

The seed of the modern vehicle ferry was first sown in Britain by the Romans as part of their mighty transport system. The legendry "Transitus Maximus", for example, provided the Humber crossing of Ermine Street; but after the Romans had left Britain in the year 411, their transport system fell into disarray. The destructive impact of the Vikings was felt when they arrived in their Longboats in 787. But it was only in the eleventh century, during the reign of King William I, that a stable commercial environment again returned sufficient for the old trading routes to be reinstated.

Rights to a ferry route were bought from the Lord of the Manor, others were granted by Royal Charter. The "Transitus Maximus" developed into a whole network of cross-Humber services, when in 1316, Edward II commanded the Burgesses of Hull to operate a ferry to carry passengers at a halfpenny each, a passenger and a horse for a penny and a cart and two horses for two pence.

Open sailing boats were in common use until the mid-eighteenth century. From then on shelter was provided for passengers, who were at last segregated from the horses, cattle and pigs. Soon the first iron ships arrived, with John Laird of Birkenhead a principal innovator, and the steam engine was also soon to put to sea.

Henry Bell had the diminutive *Comet* in service on the Clyde in 1812. Such was the success of the *Comet*, Captain James Williamson reports in his book "Clyde Passenger Steamers 1812-1901", that a further 270 steamers were put into service on the Clyde by the year 1880. Many of these ran down from the Broomielaw; most of them were owned by their Captain, who would also double as the Purser. It was not long before wheeled vehicles began to be carried on the steamers. One of the earliest references to this is given in the records of a court case held in 1877 after the Arran steamers *Glen Rosa* and *Guinevere* had collided, causing a horse to bolt and the carriage to break its tethers.

Within twenty years of the *Guinevere* incident, the first motor car was conveyed on the Clyde by the Williamson steamer *Strathmore* on a crossing to Bute. The car was loaded by means of planks laid between the pier and the ship's deck, a somewhat primitive means, but one which was to survive in many estuarine waters for a long time to come.

Meanwhile, in the south of England, the steamer *Prince Coburg* commenced a twice daily service between Southampton and Cowes in 1823. Captains Groves and Beazley introduced the *Arrow* to the Portsmouth to Ryde route at about the same time. From the 1830s onwards, goods and wheeled vehicles were carried on the Isle of Wight services in tow boats; broad barges which had removable gates for transoms. The barges were towed along by the steamer, or in later years by a special tug, and were loaded and unloaded onto a slipway. In 1885 the second-hand train ferry *Carrier* (see Chapter 2) was obtained for a cargo service between Langstone Harbour and Bembridge; but the tow boats were to labour on, both at Ryde and Lymington.

The main inhibiting factor to the development of the vehicle ferry at this time was the

Perch Rock *(Keith P. Lewis)*

nature of vehicular access between shore and deck. The planks used on the Clyde were not entirely safe, and in any case could only be used at set stages of the tide depending on the relative elevation of deck and pier. Slipways were being introduced in other parts of the country, especially in estuaries which experience a greater tidal range than the Clyde.

On the Mersey, the slipways were replaced at a very early date by floating landing stages. These were commissioned by 1884 at Seacombe, Woodside, New Brighton and Liverpool and in 1889 at Rock Ferry. Vehicular access to the Seacombe landing stage was by means of a hydraulic lift which was capable of taking two light vehicles at a time. Elsewhere floating roadways or hinged bridges were installed which allowed access for horse-drawn and motorised traffic.

It was the existence of good vehicular access to the ferries that promoted the Birkenhead Improvement Commissioners to order the very first purpose-built ferries for road vehicles. These were the so called Birkenhead "luggage boats" which were introduced from the late 1870s onwards.

The first of them was the *Oxton*, built in 1879, and she was followed a year later by the *Bebington*. They were double-ended ships with twin screws and rudders fore and aft. The main deck was completely clear apart from a central island which contained the bridge, the funnel and the ticket office. Vehicles were loaded over the side from gangways brought up from the landing stages.

The same basic design was retained for all the subsequent "luggage boats", apart from the two paddle steamers *Sunflower* and *Shamrock* (Table 1). The *Sunflower* was built in 1879 as the first Seacombe "luggage boat". However, her almost circular vehicle deck was found impractical in terms of stability and she was soon converted to a passenger only ferry. In 1891 the Wallasey Local Board purchased the ageing passenger paddle steamer *Woodside* from Birkenhead Corporation for conversion into the "luggage boat" *Shamrock*. She was not much of a success, and was withdrawn only ten years later.

A total of twelve purpose built screw driven "luggage boats" were commissioned, the last, the *Perch Rock* in 1929. Undaunted by the opening of the Mersey Railway Tunnel in 1886, their demise came soon after the Mersey Road Tunnel opened in 1934. Thereafter, there was a single ship service catering only for horse-drawn traffic and petrol wagons, both of which were prohibited from the tunnel. The Birkenhead Woodside service ceased altogether at the outbreak of World War II, but the *Perch Rock* continued on the Liverpool to Seacombe (Wallasey) service until March 1947.

The development of the steam engine is well illustrated by the "luggage boats". The first *Oxton* (1879) had a four cylinder compound expansion engine with 19 inch and 34 inch cylinders; the second *Oxton* had a six cylinder triple expansion engine with 18 inch and 28 inch cylinders.

Elsewhere the paddle steamer had become firmly established. In the early days, engines such as the steeple engine and the side lever engine were developed, but later the simple diagonal engine and the compound diagonal engine were to become the mainstay.

A landmark in vehicle and passenger ferry design was established with the decision of the London County Council to provide a free ferry at Woolwich in 1889. Two side-loading paddle steamers were constructed; named the *Duncan* and *Gordon*, they had twin two-cylinder simple condensing engines with cylinders set at right angles on a single crank. There was no coupling between the two engines and so each paddle wheel could be driven independently. This arrangement, along with the prevailing river current, allowed the vessels to crab across the river or to turn in their own length.

The ships were loaded over the side: passengers on the main deck, horses and carts and the like on the vehicle deck, which was the upper deck. Unlike the Mersey "luggage boats", the Woolwich ships were not double ended. The *Hutton*, a third identical sister was added to the service in 1893.

The pioneer trio was replaced between 1922 and 1930 by four new side loading paddlers: the *Squires*, *Gordon*, *Will Crooks* and *John Benn*, each 51 metres long and 13 metres in breadth. These ships had simple diagonal reciprocating engines which were fired by coke. They could carry 1000 passengers.

On the Tay, the paddle steamer *Newport* (310 tons gross) was the first purpose-built vehicle ferry for the Dundee Harbour Trust. She entered service between Dundee and Newport in 1910. Vehicle access was side-loading via a slipway. She was followed in 1924 by the *Sir William High* and in 1929 by the *B L Nairn*. The latter pair were sizeable ferries with gross tonnages of 311 and 395 respectively. All three ships were built at Dundee by the Caledon Shipbuilding and Engineering Company. The *Sir William High* cost £18,280 to build - her owners received £15,000 for her on her sale to a Nigerian company some 28 years later in 1924. The *B L Nairn* cost £24,000 to build; she could carry 1191 passengers and up to 26 cars.

The three Tay ferries had compound diagonal machinery with independently driven paddle wheels. The sponsons were carried all the way from bow to stern so that a full width deck was available to facilitate loading and to allow the carriage of up to 30 cars on the foredeck. The after part of the main deck was given over to a large passenger saloon. The *Newport* was withdrawn in 1941, whereas the younger pair were only withdrawn in the early 1950s.

In 1939 the diesel driven *Abercraig* was built for the service by Fleming & Ferguson at Paisley at a cost of £55,000. She was fitted with the brand new Voith Schneider propellers from Germany, one unit at the bows and one at the stern. She was joined by a near sister, the *Scotscraig*, in 1950. The second ship was built at the Caledon yard at Dundee, and the post-war cost had risen to £171,000. The gross tonnage of the two ferries was respectively 455 and 463; they could carry 1200 passengers and 45 cars. The Voith Schneider system allows directional thrust to overcome the need for a rudder, and provides a far greater degree of control than conventional systems particularly when operating in confined waters (see page 78).

The North and South Queensferry service on the Forth also operated from a pair of slipways. Until 1934 it was maintained by paddle steamers including the ancient *Dundee*, which was originally built for the Dundee to Newport service in 1875 at a cost of £8970 by William Simons & Company at Renfrew. The paddle steamers could carry up to ten cars on their foredecks - not an altogether comfortable arrangement.

In 1934 two identical sisters were commissioned for the Forth crossing. These were the *Queen Margaret* and the *Robert the Bruce*; 49 metres long by 15 metres broad they had a gross tonnage of 228. The idea to build the two ferries came from a suggestion by Sir Maurice Denny the shipbuilder to the then operator, the London and North Eastern Railway Company. The railway company countered that Denny should not only build the ferries, but that he should also operate them. This he did and the ferries entered service for William Denny & Brothers Limited, shipbuilders and ferry managers of Dumbarton.

The ships were double ended. They were able to load 28 cars over the side onto the adjacent slipway via ramps hinged off the deck of the ship. Their machinery was quite novel for the time; a sixteen cylinder oil engine was coupled to an electric generator and motor system in order to reduce the high revolutions of the engine to an acceptable speed for the paddles. Diesel-electric propulsion had been tried earlier, for example in the David MacBrayne screw ship *Lochfyne* of 1930.

Paddle steamers also ruled the roost on the Hull to New Holland crossing of the Humber. Wheeled vehicles were loaded off a sloping slipway-like pier at New Holland by crane, and again craned-off at the other side. Hinged roadways to floating stages were installed ready for the arrival of the two majestic paddle ferries the *Wingfield Castle* and *Tattershall Castle* which were completed in 1934 by William Gray & Company of West Hartlepool for the London and North Eastern Railway Company. (The builders were not invited to operate this service!)

The two sisters were coal burning with triple expansion diagonal engines which gave them a service speed of 13 knots. They were 61 metres long and 17 metres across the paddle boxes. They were unique as British paddle steamers with the funnel placed aft of the paddles. Their capacity was a substantial 556 tons gross. They could carry up to 1200

Wingfield Castle *(Nick Robins)*

passengers and 20 cars, the latter loaded over ramps on the landing stages which connected to the after part of the sponson.

A third ferry, the Clyde-built *Lincoln Castle* joined the earlier pair in 1940. She was slightly larger at 598 tons gross and conformed by having her funnel forward of the paddle boxes. Her delivery voyage was abandoned due to compass failure and it was a whole year before the war effort allowed a second and successful attempt to be made in 1941. A most memorable feature of the three Humber ferries was the small railway style buffet situated below the main lounge. This small muggy haven provided passengers with large steaming cups of tea and doorstep-sandwiches during the 20 minute voyage.

Screw propelled vehicle ferries also flourished, particularly in riverine waters which had a fast tidal current. Such is the case in the Thames between Tilbury and Gravesend. Here the vehicle ferry *Tessa* was introduced in 1924 and her sister the *Mimie* followed in 1927. They were coal burners, the *Tessa* was built on the Ribble at Lytham, whereas the *Mimie* was a product of Ferguson's at Port Glasgow. The *Tessa* was the smaller of the two at 368 tons gross, being some 43 metres long by 12 metres broad. They could load 25 to 30 cars over the side, fore and aft of the central island, using ramps to connect with the respective landing stages.

The concept of end-loading over the slipway via ramps hinged from the bow and stern could only be realised by some means of steadying the vessel alongside the slipway. This could be an adjacent pier against which the ship could tie up or nowadays hold herself in position under her own power, or it could be via guide ropes.

The guide-rope principal was adopted for the *Dartmouth Higher Ferry*, built in

Dartmouth in 1920. A paddle steamer driven by coal-fired compound diagonal engines she was led from one slipway to the other by parallel guide wires. She could carry only 12 cars but she was one of the first drive-through ferries in British waters. The wheel-house was placed on the opposite side of the ship to the funnel and she was always positioned with the funnel upstream due to the prevailing winds.

The guide-rope principle developed into the chain ferry, whereby the propulsion unit on the ferry is coupled to wheels which grip the chain, and the ferry literally pulls itself along to the opposite slipway. There were and are many examples of this method including the one-time Southampton Floating Bridge and the present day Sandbanks Ferry across the mouth of Poole Harbour.

There were some odd ferry systems. At Finnieston in Glasgow, the *Vehicular Ferry* completed her 100 metre traverse of the River Clyde by lifting her entire vehicle deck up beneath a fixed gallows-like structure until vehicles could drive off onto the roadway. This particular service lasted from its inauguration at the turn of the century until 1966.

The archaic tow-boats on the Isle of Wight services were finally displaced with the introduction of the twin-screw motor vessels *Fishbourne, Wootton* and *Hilsea* by the Southern Railway Company in 1927, 1928 and 1930 respectively. Although they were small, varying from 149 to 156 tons gross, they were original in design and very much a landmark in car ferry architecture. They ran between the Broad Street Slip at Portsmouth and the new Fishbourne Slipway at Wootton Creek, near Ryde.

The new ferries had hinged ramps at bow and stern which were used to load wheeled vehicles off the slipway. The ramps could cope with loads of up to eight tons. The ferries could carry 18 cars and 100 passengers. They were truly double ended, being motor ships, with twin screws and twin rudders at each end. The bridge structure straddled the vehicle deck leaving it completely uncluttered. The ships were a huge success; their reliability in service on a relatively exposed stretch of water proved that bow and stern-hinged doors could have a wider use beyond estuarine waters.

A fourth drive-through car ferry was ordered by the Southern Railway Company in 1938; this was the equally innovative double ended motor ferry *Lymington*, which like the new Tay ferry *Abercraig*, was fitted with Voith Schneider propulsion.

The *Lymington* could accommodate 20 cars and 400 passengers. She operated from the narrow channel of the Lymington River to Yarmouth on the Isle of Wight. By today's standards she was tiny, with a capacity of only 275 tons gross, she was 45 metres long and 11 metres broad, but she was the forerunner of a design that was to be copied repeatedly in later years. At the beginning of World War II the *Lymington* represented the state of the art in estuarine ferries.

THE COMPOUND ENGINE AND THE TRIPLE EXPANSION ENGINE

The compound steam reciprocating engine was introduced as higher boiler pressures became available. The boiler steam is admitted to one cylinder only where it is half expanded, then it is allowed into the other cylinder at reduced pressure and finally exhausted to the condenser. In this form of double expansion compound engine both the high pressure cylinder and the low pressure cylinder drive onto their own crank. A diagonal compound engine is one where the cylinders are at the bottom of the engine and inclined at about 20 degrees from the horizontal pointing at the crank shaft. In the diagonal engine the piston rods plunge up and down sloping guides.

The triple expansion engine was developed as even higher steam pressures became available. In this engine the compounding process was extended to a third stage, whereby the second cylinder exhausted into a third cylinder before the spent steam was passed on to the condenser. The three cylinders were called the high pressure, intermediate pressure and low pressure cylinders. They each drove independent cranks usually set at 120 degrees from each other.

The condenser has two functions. It firstly condenses the steam back into water which can be returned to the boiler, and secondly it creates a negative pressure at the exhaust end of the engine so releasing the maximum amount of energy from the steam. This is because it is the actual expansion of the steam in the closed cylinders which does the work, and not the pressure of the steam.

TABLE 1. THE MERSEY "LUGGAGE BOATS"

Name	Built	Sold	Gross Tons	Length (m)	Breadth (m)	Comments
Birkenhead						
Oxton (I)	1879	1930	431	40	14	Renamed *Old Oxton* 1925
Bebington (I)	1880	1927	435	40	14	Renamed *Old Bebington* 1925
Tranmere	1884	1925	435	40	14	
Barnston	1921	1939	724	44	15	
Churnton	1921	1939	724	44	15	
Bebington (II)	1925	1949	732	44	15	
Oxton (II)	1925	1949	732	44	15	
Seacombe						
Sunflower	1879	1905	345	43	8	Paddle Steamer
Wallasey	1881	1925	459	43	14	
Shamrock	1865	1901	589	46	10	Paddle Steamer. Ex-passenger ferry 1891
Seacombe	1901	1929	589	43	15	
Liscard	1921	1948	734	45	15	
Leasowe	1921	1948	734	45	15	
Perch Rock	1929	1953	766	44	15	

CHAPTER 2

TRAIN FERRIES

The world's very first train ferry was the *Leviathan*, which entered service between Granton near Edinburgh and Burntisland in Fife on 7th February 1850. She was followed a year later by a sister, the *Robert Napier*, which was named after the builder of the two ferries. The *Robert Napier*, which had a capacity of 216 tons gross, took up service alongside the passenger only paddle steamer *Express* between Ferryport-on-Craig and Broughty Ferry on the Tay.

The two train ferries were an integral part of the Edinburgh, Perth and Dundee Railway Company's line which ran from Burntisland via Cupar to Ferryport-on-Craig. So successful were they at the transhipment of goods rail wagons that a third slightly larger train ferry, the *Carrier* of 243 tons gross, was built in 1858 to supplement the Tay crossing. The ships had two rail tracks side by side along the main deck. They were double ended and could carry goods wagons with a total weight of 140 tons, the wagons being shunted onto the ferries via a slipway arrangement. They did not carry passengers.

In 1861 the two ferry services became part of the mighty North British Railway Company, but plans were soon drawn up for the construction of a railway bridge across the Tay. The first train crossed the new Tay Bridge in May 1878, allowing the displaced ferries to assist in a two ship service at Burntisland with one spare ship - but not for long.

The collapse of the bridge in awful weather conditions on the night of 28th December only seven months later, and with the loss of about 70 lives, saw the *Robert Napier* reinstated on the Tay. The opening of the present railway bridge across the Tay in June 1887 again displaced the ferry to the Forth, but three years later the Forth Railway Bridge was opened and the need for that train ferry service also ceased. The respective passenger ferry services (later also with vehicle ferries - Chapter 1) nevertheless continued. The two older train ferries were scrapped, but the *Carrier* which had become spare ship at Granton in 1882, had been sold via an Edinburgh company in 1884 to the Marine Transit Company Limited of London. She was then used as a vehicle ferry to the Isle of Wight (Chapter 1) and was eventually scrapped in 1893.

By the turn of the century, train ferries had become an important component of the North American railway system, where they offered a cheaper capital outlay than a bridge on many non-tidal crossings. In Europe the first sea going train ferry services started in the Baltic before the Great War. The pioneer was the *Drottning Victoria* which took four hours to make the 95 kilometre crossing between Sassnitz in Germany and Trelleborg in Sweden. The ship was 113 metres long and could accommodate a whole passenger train, comprising eight 22 metre long coaches, on twin rail tracks.

The first British-flag sea-going train ferries were the *Train Ferry No 1*, *Train Ferry No 2* and the *Train Ferry No 3*, all built in 1917 by Armstrong Whitworth at Newcastle. The ships were 111 metres long by 18 metres broad with a capacity of 2755 tons gross. They had oil fired-triple expansion engines and twin screws, which drove the ships at a service speed of 12 knots. Placed in service as Ministry of War Transports at Richborough in Kent, their main purpose was to support the war effort on the Continent. At Richborough they berthed in the River Stour

***Suffolk Ferry** (Nick Robins)*

alongside the railway line beneath Richborough Castle, just up-river from the town of Sandwich. Access to the berth was by means of a by-pass channel which had been cut across the large meander in the river on which Sandwich stands. The main Continental terminal was Dunkerque.

The main deck was open aft, and two rail tracks ran forward over the stern and divided into four tracks for almost the full length of the ships. The main deck was uncluttered as the funnels were positioned at either side of the ship. Loading was by means of a twin track draw-bridge, lowered from the shore, and locked onto a pin at the stern of the ferry. The Continental rail gauge was (and is), for the most part, compatible with our own but the Continental rail wagons did not conform to the British loading gauge; only UK built army wagons could be used on the service. Each ship was capable of unloading and loading a full complement of 54 ten tonne trucks in just one hour.

With Europe again at peace the military need for the service declined. However, in the words of the Wonder Book of Ships, Fourteenth Edition (undated but probably published between 1930 and 1932):

"The War showed that a train service across the Channel must be established and maintained whatever the weather, and the train ferries between Richborough and France, when once started, were kept up regularly. The saving of time in the transport of war material was of the greatest importance, financially and nationally."

In 1924 the service forsook its awkward harbour at Richborough and moved to Harwich under the auspices of the Great Eastern Train Ferry Company. A purpose-built siding was built beyond Harwich Town Station, and a twin track pier and draw-bridge built into the river at Old Harwich. The Continental terminal became Zeebrugge, although some services initially ran to Dunkerque.

The service flourished as through-wagons could be consigned to many countries, but excluding Russia, Portugal and Spain whose railways did not use the otherwise universal 4 feet 8 1/2 inch gauge. In 1934 the three train ferries became part of the London & North Eastern Railway Company.

Only the *Train Ferry No 1* survived the Second World War. She was converted to the Landing Ship *Iris* in 1940 and renamed HMS *Princess Iris* in 1942. During the war she often had a complement of 200 men. She was returned to railway service in 1946 and given the name *Essex Ferry* following a major refit during which she also acquired a single funnel amidships in place of her original twin pole funnels. She became the *Essex Ferry II* in 1956, before she was scrapped in 1957; a pioneer and a grand old lady.

The *Train Ferry No 2* was an early casualty in the war, being beached and abandoned at Le Havre on 12th January 1940. The *Train Ferry No 3* became the train ferry *Daffodil* during the war, which she almost survived, but she was lost on 18th March 1945 after contact with a mine the previous day. During the aftermath of the D Day landings in the summer and autumn of 1944, a number of Type 2 Landing Ships Tank were equipped with railway tracks in order to ferry rail wagons between Southampton and Cherbourg. Railway engines could not, however, gain access due to the limited space between the bow doors (see Chapter 5).

Back in November 1930 the Southern Railway Company had resolved to introduce a cross-Channel passenger train ferry between Dover and Boulogne, although Dunkerque was eventually selected as the Continental terminal on advice from the French. In April 1933 a tender was awarded to Swan Hunter & Wigham Richardson on the Tyne for three ferries each

***Shepperton Ferry** (FotoFlite)*

Cambridge Ferry *(Nick Robins)*

110 metres long by 19 metres broad. The ships were to be equipped with coal-fired steam turbine machinery and twin screws. The three ships were all launched during 1933: the first named *Twickenham Ferry* on 15th March, second, the *Hampton Ferry* on 30th July and the third, the *Shepperton Ferry* on 23rd October.

Delivered between March and July 1935 the three ships were found to have an alarming tendency to roll. Each received an additional 200 tonnes of ballast in the form of old railway lines. Meanwhile a special train ferry dock was being constructed at Dover in which a constant water level could be maintained despite the 8 metre range in tide within Dover Harbour. This would allow the loading of passenger coaches via a twin track draw-bridge regardless of the tide. Geological problems severely delayed the project, and it was found that the permeability of fractures in the Chalk allowed the dock to drain back to the sea faster than the pumps could pump the level up! The engineering problems finally overcome, the ships eventually commenced the service on 6th October 1936.

Immediately before the service started the *Twickenham Ferry* was transferred to the French flag in lieu of three French ships which the new ferries displaced. The *Twickenham Ferry* took the first inbound service and the *Hampton Ferry* the first outbound service. The *Shepperton Ferry* followed into service in November after adjustments had been made to her bow rudder.

The ships could accommodate up to 700 passengers and could carry either 12 "wagons lits" or 40 standard-type goods trucks. Beyond the stern, the twin rail tracks divided into four. There was also a small upper deck garage for the carriage of 25 cars. The famous "Night Ferry" was initially run between London and Paris, but in post-war years the train was divided and Brussels also became a destination. The "Night Ferry" left either port in the early hours of the morning.

The service was suspended on 25th August 1939 when the *Hampton Ferry* and *Shepperton*

Ferry were requisitioned as the minelayers HMS *Hampton* and HMS *Shepperton* respectively. Both were returned to civilian duties within a year and were principally used on the Larne to Stranraer service for the remainder of the war. At the end of the war the ships were converted from coal to oil burning. The Dover train ferry was restarted in December 1947 by the *Shepperton Ferry*, followed shortly afterwards by her two sisters. New tonnage was added at Dover in 1951 when the French flag *Saint Germain* joined the service.

The *Hampton Ferry* moved to Stranraer in June 1953 following the loss of the *Princess Victoria* (see Chapter 4). At Stranraer the *Hampton Ferry* operated alongside the passenger ship *Princess Margaret* of 1931, offering a vehicle ferry service, mornings from Stranraer and evenings out of Larne. She returned to Dover in the Autumn of 1961. The *Shepperton Ferry* also came to the short sea route as relief for the *Caledonian Princess* during the early 1960s.

New tonnage was also badly needed at Harwich due to war losses. The first of the new Harwich ships was the *Suffolk Ferry*, built at John Brown & Company at Clydebank. She had a capacity of 3134 gross tons. A near sister, the *Norfolk Ferry* was also built at Clydebank, she had a capacity of 3157 gross tons and arrived on station in 1951. Their dimensions were slightly larger than the original trio built in 1917. The new ships were diesel powered, and the main visual difference between them was that the *Suffolk Ferry* carried a larger funnel than her sister.

The Harwich train ferry thrived. The old *Essex Ferry* was replaced by a ship of the same name in 1956. The new *Essex Ferry* was built to the same basic design as the post war twins and had a capacity of 3242 gross tons. The three ferries served the Harwich route without incident, and in 1963 a fourth ship, the *Cambridge Ferry* entered service. She was similar in many respects with a gross tonnage of 3294, but sported a tapered funnel and streamlined bridge-housing.

Increased demand for the service was now satisfied. Three ship continuity was maintained throughout the overhaul periods, whilst at other times the spare fourth ship rode the buoys off

Anderida *(Nick Robins)*

***Vortigern** (Miles Cowsill)*

Parkeston Quay. Each ship could carry twelve passengers, and had the standard arrangement of twin tracks over the stern widening to four over much of the length of the ship. Up to 38 International Rail Wagons could be carried although road trailers were to become a significant part of the load as time went on.

In 1977 the *Cambridge Ferry* received a major refit. This included the extension of her boat deck aft in order to accommodate export cars, and modifications to her stern which enabled her to operate additionally to Dunkerque. The *Norfolk Ferry* was also modified.

New tonnage was considered in 1980 and plans were made to build two large train ferries, the first for delivery in 1983, the second in 1985. As a temporary measure the *Stena Shipper* was taken on charter and given the name *Speedlink Vanguard.* She was registered at London, although the other four ships were all registered at Harwich, and a £4 million refit was carried out during which rail tracks were fitted to her two main cargo decks.

The arrival of the *Speedlink Vanguard* coincided with a down-turn in traffic and the *Suffolk Ferry* was peremptorily sold for demolition at Antwerp. By 1982 both the *Norfolk Ferry* and the *Essex Ferry* were laid up, plans for new-building were abandoned, and the charter of *Speedlink Vanguard* was unexpectedly renewed.

The *Cambridge Ferry* had been occupied on the new Harwich to Dunkerque service, but this ceased in April 1982 reducing her to stand-by duties. During the following winter she returned to the Zeebrugge route after a brief spell of service out of Dover. That same winter the *Speedlink Vanguard* collided with, and sank the Townsend Thoresen freighter *European Gateway* off Felixstowe (see Chapter 14). Damage to the train ferry was slight, however, and she was soon back on service.

In 1983 the *Essex Ferry* was sold for use in salvage work in Norway after being partly demolished to train deck level at Rainham, Kent and the *Norfolk Ferry* was sold for demolition at Flushing. The Harwich to Zeebrugge service finally closed in January 1987. The *Speedlink Vanguard* was returned to Stena Line, but the *Cambridge Ferry* became a nomadic support ship, firstly at Dover and later on all the Irish Sea trailer services, only being sold in 1992.

At Dover the three pre-war passenger and train ferries and the *Saint Germain* continued until 1969 when the multi-purpose train and vehicle ferry *Vortigern* was introduced. The *Vortigern* had a capacity of 4371 gross tons and was some 114 metres long by 19 metres breadth. She could carry 1000 passengers and had room for 240 cars or 366 lane-metres of freight vehicles. Her design speed was 16 knots for the overnight train ferry run to Dunkerque and 20 knots for the car ferry service to Boulogne. Her arrival displaced the *Hampton Ferry* which was eventually sold.

In August 1972 the ageing *Shepperton Ferry* was replaced by the new freight and train ferry *Anderida.* Built by the Trasvik shipyard in Brevik in Norway, she was adopted as a train ferry at a late stage of her construction. The French flag multi-purpose ship *Saint Eloi* joined the service in 1975, replacing the *Twickenham Ferry* which had been scrapped in 1973. The *Saint Eloi* continued on the train ferry service between Dover and Dunkerque until 1988 when she was transferred to the Dover-Calais car ferry service. Renamed the *Channel Entente* in 1989 she was sold to the Isle of Man Steam Packet Company in 1990 to become the *King Orry*, flying the Red Ensign from 1995 onwards.

In 1978 the SNCF freight ferry *Transcontainer 1* was converted for rail traffic for use at either Dover or Harwich. At the same time the *Vortigern* was used almost entirely on the car ferry service to Boulogne, and consequently, her "A" Deck garage, capable of taking 40 cars and situated above the main train deck, was converted into a passenger lounge and her passenger certificate was increased to 1350.

The *Vortigern* was not a trouble free ship. In June 1970 she struck an uncharted object which was thought at the time to be a submarine and was off service for several months. In January 1981, whilst on passage between Ostend and Folkestone, she suffered an engine room fire which caused considerable electrical damage. Her greatest ignominy occurred in the morning of 4th March 1982 when she went ashore across a stone groyne on a falling tide at Ostend. She was pulled off two days later. Had she not been built with a strengthened hull for the carriage of trains she might well not have survived. She was eventually sold into the Greek registry in 1988.

In 1987 the Dover Train Ferry Dock fell into disuse with the opening of the new No 5 Berth on the Admiralty Pier. The train ferry service became the preserve of a new and larger ship, the French flag *Nord Pas de Calais.* The era of the "Night Ferry" was over and that of Eurostar had begun; the opening of the Channel Tunnel placed the future of this last remaining train ferry in jeopardy and the service ceased at the end of 1995.

When the fleet Commodore Captain John Arthur retired in 1981 he commented that his all time favourite command had been the *Shepperton Ferry.* With her large windage and inadequate power she had taught him a great deal about ship handling. "That class of ship either made you or broke you", he said.

CHAPTER 3

STUART TOWNSEND AND THE SOUTHERN RAILWAY COMPANY

The provision of cross-channel train ferries was a logical way for the British railway companies to extend their rail networks onto the Continent. These companies were also quite happy to reap the profits from the provision of passenger steamers which linked UK and Continental railway terminals, and from cargo steamers which carried the goods. They did not, however, wish to encourage the eccentric fringe who, forsaking the trains, insisted on travelling overland by motor car, both at home and abroad.

The Southern Railway Company was formed in 1923. At that time the standard of service on the Dover Strait had been allowed to fall to a low ebb with the thirteen elderly cross-Channel passenger and cargo ships of the South Eastern and Chatham Railway Company. The Southern Railway Company undertook to rebuild the image of the French connection by building one new ship for the Dover Strait for each of the first twelve years of the new company's existence. This they did, but throughout this massive capital programme, the provision for the carriage of cars and their drivers was all but neglected.

The one concession made by the Southern Railway Company was the decision in 1930 to modify the design of the seventh cargo ship to be completed for the Dover station in order that it could carry cars. The first six cargo ships carried town names (the *Tonbridge*, *Minster*, *Hythe*, *Whitstable*, *Maidstone* and *Deal*), but not the new ship, which emerged with the hybrid name *Autocarrier* and not the *Camberley* as had been planned.

Built by D W Henderson of Glasgow for £49976, the *Autocarrier* was launched on the 5th February 1931 and arrived at Dover with a cargo of Scottish coal on 26th March 1931. She commenced her daily service between Dover and Calais five days later. She was small for the intended purpose and had a capacity of only 822 tons gross, and a length of 67 metres. She was coal fired and her engines maintained a service speed of 15 knots. She carried up to 35 cars, which were loaded and off-loaded in slings beneath a crane; she offered accommodation for 120 drivers and their passengers. The single fare for a car was £5/15/0d on the mail boats and a very modest £2 on the *Autocarrier*.

What had forced the railway company with their monopoly to make this generous concession to the motorist? It was the result of one of the earliest examples of consumer power, brought about when just one disgruntled Englishman with a sick wife in France had to travel repeatedly across the Channel with his motor car in order to visit her. The motorist was a Mr Stuart D Townsend, whose family firm of Townsend Brothers was involved in ship management and ship delivery.

Mr Townsend was so appalled with the service and conditions offered to motorists by the Southern Railway Company that he chartered his own ship to provide a competitive service. At this time, cars were, of course, craned aboard and petrol tanks drained, the shore gang had to be tipped, and damage caused to the vehicle whilst in transit had to be tolerated. Besides all this the railway company, believing that all motorists must by definition be wealthy, charged a high fare. In an attempt to persuade the Southern Railway Company to reform their attitude towards the motorist, Stuart Townsend took the steam coaster *Artificer* on a one month charter in July 1928.

The *Artificer* carried 15 crane-loaded cars and up to 12 passengers, other passengers were taken by bus to the Admiralty Pier and put on the mail steamer. The service was the very first to be based in the Eastern corner of Dover Harbour; the *Artificer* berthed alongside the Eastern Arm in the old Camber Dock which is now reclaimed. The passage time to Calais was two and a half hours, but even so, there was a clear demand from drivers to accompany their cars on the extended crossing, rather than assume the relative comfort of the mail steamer. The single fare was £2 and the return fare was £3/15/0d (cf the current summer period fares of between £100 and £130 single and £175 and £225 return).

So successful was the charter that the *Artificer* was retained throughout the winter until she was replaced by another charter in the form of the slightly larger *Royal Firth*. Profit on the first year of trading was £80. At this point the railway company chartered the small coasters *Abington* and *Dublin* and put them in tandem with the Dover mail steamer, and employed the *Whitstable* for the same purpose at Folkestone. They too reduced their fare to only £2; the first price war on the Channel had begun. Competition from the railway company forced Townsend to withdraw his service for the following winter (1929/30), by which time the Southern Railway Company had come down to a single fare for a car of only £1-17-6d.

During the Autumn of 1929 Townsend bought the minesweeper HMS *Ford* from the Admiralty for £5000 with plans, prepared by Mr Norman Dewar, to convert her into a stern-loading car ferry. The ship was returned to her builders, Earles Shipbuilding & Engineering Company of Hull, from where she emerged the following spring as the car ferry *Forde* with Hull as her port of registry.

In the words of Stuart Townsend:

"Right from the beginning I had appreciated that passengers would prefer to drive their cars onto a ship rather than see them lifted by crane and get palpitations in case they dropped from mid-air. Hence I long urged upon the port authorities on both sides of the Channel the desirability of installing adjustable bridges, and even when the Forde was being converted for the ferry service I had her fitted with a loading gate at the stern."

The *Forde* had been completed in 1919. She was a coal burner and her triple expansion engines could drive her at 18 knots. Unfortunately the Board of Trade imposed limitations on her boiler pressure as a merchant ship and her operational speed was a modest 13 knots. She had room for 200 passengers and 30 cars, and she commenced duty between Dover and Calais on 15th April 1930. The absence of loading bridges at both ports prevented her from using her stern ramp, but both the Dover and Calais port authorities promised to rectify this. In the mean time, cars, buses and even lorries continued to be loaded and unloaded by crane.

It was this situation that had led the Southern Railway Company to complete the new *Camberley* as the *Autocarrier*. This ship entered service one year after the *Forde*, but for the next six years the two ferries battled it out, the *Forde* operating the summer season only, but both ships making an uneconomical return with the depressed fares until a pooling arrangement was finally agreed in 1937. Only then were the fares elevated to an economic level and a profit returned to their two respective owners.

The French General Strike in June 1936 at last allowed the *Forde* to demonstrate the value of her stern gates. Turning her stern onto the quayside, vehicles were driven straight onto the ship at the appropriate point in the tide and the need for a strike-bound shore crane was obviated. This respite, which allowed her to use her drive-on facility, was all too brief, as the strike was soon over and there were still no adjustable bridges provided at either port.

During the war years the *Forde* was used as a salvage ship, although she was found to be a bit too light in construction for this kind of work. She returned to service as a car ferry after the war but lasted only until October 1949, receiving her cargo by crane to the very end.

The competitor, the *Autocarrier*, was used in the war as a welfare ship based at Lyness in Orkney. In December 1945 she was released back to her owners who initially employed her between Southampton and Alderney repatriating the islanders, and then on the Channel Islands to Grouville and St Malo service until the miniature cross-Channel steamer *Brittany* returned from the war on 6th June 1946. The *Autocarrier* then reopened the passenger link to Le Havre on 13th January 1947 until she was again displaced by the *Brittany* which in turn was displaced by the *Hantonia* in June of the same year. Her cattle pens were then removed and her crow's nest taken down and she moved to the Folkestone to Boulogne cargo service until she was sold for demolition in 1954. In the immediate post-war years it was realised that she was too small to resume her car ferry duties at Dover, whereupon the *Dinard* was taken in hand for conversion for this service (see Chapter 6).

The replacement for Townsend's *Forde* was the two year old River-class frigate HMS *Halladale*, which was bought for £15,000 in 1948. Unlike HMS *Ford* which gained the letter "e" on conversion, the *Halladale* was able to retain her original name.

Stuart Townsend's son David wrote (Sea Breezes December 1976):

The Halladale entered service in 1950, and for her conversion Mr Norman Dewar had again prepared the plans, also supervised the work being carried out; this was done by the Cork Dockyard Company, who quoted a fixed price for the job (£77,000). I had been determined not to award the contract on a cost-plus basis. Her original builders were A & J Inglis, and she had a length of 92 metres, a beam of 11 metres and a gross tonnage of 1370. The engines were twin screw turbines. Her capacity was 55 cars and 368 passengers, and speed 20 knots.

She entered service on 6th April 1950, but following grounding damage four days later, the service was suspended until 19th May.

It was the *Halladale* that finally realised Stuart Townsend's dream, as it was she that became the first cross (English) Channel drive-on drive-off ferry. Townsend had managed to buy a redundant Callender Hamilton Bailey-type bridge in 1946 and this was duly installed at Berth 3 in Calais Harbour. Use of the bridge to facilitate loading was inaugurated by the *Halladale* on 27th June 1951. Meanwhile at Dover, twin linkspans were built and opened at the Dover Eastern Docks terminal on 30th June 1953; the *Halladale* had actually been using the linkspans when they first became available earlier on in the year and was again the very first ship to use this new facility.

It is interesting to note that linkspans had been introduced at Stranraer and Larne before the war. The Continental train ferries, of course, had used this same principle since 1917, and drive-through ferries, not just stern loading ferries, were first introduced in the Baltic in the 1920s. It took the Dover and Calais port authorities until the early 1950s to realise Stuart Townsend's far-sighted vision of a drive-on, drive-off service, a vision which the *Forde* was never to enjoy. Nevertheless, the stern gate of the *Forde* was used on at least two occasions in addition to the General Strike at Calais - at the pleasure of passengers who preferred to lose their cars at sea rather than confront Customs at the end of the crossing!

The *Halladale* continued until 1961 when she was sold for further service in Finland and later in Venezuela. By 1957 Townsend Car Ferries Ltd. had been taken over by George Nott Industries, but by the end of her career with the firm, the *Halladale* had carried an estimated one million passengers and over a quarter of a million cars. The old Bailey bridge linkspan at Calais outlived the ferry and remained in use until 1980.

CARS ACROSS THE CHANNEL

From an article by David Townsend which first appeared in Sea Breezes, December, 1976

In the following passage the author is quoting his father Stuart Townsend:

There was one incident during the first month that the *Forde* was on the Calais run, something went wrong when she was approaching the quay there and she collided with it head on. I happened to be lunching when a messenger came running in to say the ship was sinking. I hoped that I put on a successful imitation of the phlegmatic Englishman by refusing to leave the table. Anyhow, the *Forde* did not sink, but she did sustain sufficient damage to put her out of commission for a month.

Within the year something of the same kind occurred at Dover, but this time it was the stern that suffered. Undoubtedly it was through a mistake in the engine room, probably a faulty reading of the telegraph. I devised an apparatus for preventing such a thing happening again, an alarm which would sound if, for instance, an attempt was made to put the engines astern when the telegraph showed ahead. .After much brain-work in evolving the circuit, which took in the reversing gear and the engine room telegraph, I discovered that the same device was already patented, so we settled for buying an outfit from the licensees. No further accident of the same kind ever happened.

We nearly had one of another sort, however, when the British Railways *Dinard* overtook the *Forde* in the entrance to Dover Harbour. As a result of it I suggested to the Harbour Board that every ship coming in should have a number, and that this number should be displayed from the signal station to make clear which one was to enter. The system in use was to hoist a shape when the entrance was clear for incoming ships, but this did not prevent two from entering together.

The *Halladale*, too, had her incidents. During the first season she got out of control leaving Calais and struck a camber with her bows, damaging the bow rudder and the stem. On another occasion she collided with a German coaster when leaving Dover: the coaster was in charge of a local pilot and was entering the harbour against the signals.

A further accident was in Dover Harbour itself, when the *Halladale* was stopped ready to go astern into her berth and the Belgian car ferry *Prinses Josephine Charlotte* ran into her, but on this occasion only slight damage was caused and the service not interrupted.

CHAPTER 4

THE PRINCESSES VICTORIA

The first British-flag, purpose built, sea going drive-on drive-off car and passenger ferry was built to the order of the London, Midland and Scottish Railway Company for their Stranraer to Larne service. The ship was named *Princess Victoria*; she entered service on 7th July 1939, just before the outbreak of World War II. Her pedigree was sound, she was the third ship of the name to operate on the crossing (Table 2) but she was otherwise a first in every way.

The sisters *Princess Maud* and *Princess Margaret* had maintained the route since their own introduction to service in 1931 and 1934 respectively. During the 1930s there was a sustained growing demand for the carriage of motor vehicles, livestock and general goods and in 1934 approximately 2000 cars used the crossing. Indeed by 1938 219,000 passengers were carried, but so were 20,000 tons of goods, 75,000 animals and an incredible 5450 cars. It was these statistics which persuaded the railway company to build the *Princess Victoria* as a replacement for one of the two, still very young, passenger mail ships.

The new car ferry was built by Denny of Dumbarton, as were six of her predecessors. Launched in April 1939, she had a capacity of 2197 tons gross, and was 98 metres long by 15 metres broad. The "Floating Garage" as she was called, could accommodate 1400 passengers and 80 cars; the cars were loaded through a stern door onto the car deck where there was only 4 metres headroom. Vehicular access to the shore at both terminals was by way of specially constructed hinged loading ramps which were landed onto the ships deck once the stern gate was opened. There was no need for a special tide-free dock like the Dover Train Ferry Dock because the tidal range in the northern Irish Sea is only 4 metres and road vehicles are less susceptible to gradient.

Another first for the ship was her propulsion machinery; she was the first sea-going railway company ship to be equipped with diesel engines. Not a novelty in itself, as the *Ulster Monarch* and sisters of the Belfast Steamship Company were diesel driven (and they each had two funnels!) and the last three Belgian mail ships of the 1930s also had diesel engines.

The arrival in service of the new car ferry displaced the *Princess Margaret* to Holyhead, leaving the *Princess Maud* as the running mate. Both the passenger ships were built as coal burners but were converted during the war to use oil. The *Princess Victoria* was scheduled to depart from Stranraer at 1900 hours and Larne at 1000 hours, with the mail ship leaving Stranraer at 0600 hours and Larne at 1900 hours. This cosy arrangement lasted precisely two months; as war was once again declared, both ships were immediately requisitioned and the *Princess Margaret* was sent back to maintain the service.

The state-of-the-art car ferry *Princess Victoria* gave her owners two months operational service before she was ignominiously converted into a minelayer. She served well in her new capacity, carrying mines on her car deck for discharge through the stern door. Nevertheless she met an early end off the Humber when she struck an enemy acoustic mine, and sank between 18th and 19th May 1940. She had been returning home from a foray along the German coast; thirty four of her crew lost their lives. Only two weeks later, on 30th May 1940, a shell landed

***Princess Victoria* (1946)** *(University of Glasgow Business Record Centre)*

in the engine room of the *Princess Maud* while she was off Gravelines during the evacuation of Dunkerque. A number of the engine room staff were killed in this incident, but the steamer herself was to survive the war.

The war effort required intensive exchange of military personnel, along with their tanks and other heavy wheeled equipment, between Northern Ireland and Scotland. This service was admirably provided, via the loading ramps which had been built for the *Princess Victoria*, by the Dover train ferries *Hampton Ferry*, *Shepperton Ferry* and *Twickenham Ferry* (see Chapter 2).

At the cessation of hostilities the *Princess Maud* resumed service at Stranraer for a short period prior to leaving for Holyhead in September 1946, at which time the *Princess Margaret* resumed. Steps had already been taken by the railway company to replace the lost car ferry. She was to be another *Princess Victoria* with exactly the same hull shape and dimensions as her pre-war namesake. Another product of William Denny's yard, she was launched on 26th August 1946. Her gross tonnage was slightly larger than the earlier ship at 2694, and she could carry 100 more passengers, although her garage could accommodate only 40 cars. The new *Princess Victoria* took up service in March 1947; she adopted the same summer roster as the pre-war car ferry had done in 1939, but she took over the mail service roster in the winter months.

Outwardly the two ships differed very little. In fact from the beam, they looked like any other Denny-built passenger ferry of that era, but from astern the low car deck gate gave her away for a car and passenger ferry. The low gate resembled those characteristic of the Dover and Harwich train ferries rather than the conventional stern door we know today.

Princess Victoria vehicle deck(*University of Glasgow Business Record Centre)*

In her first years of service, the new *Princess Victoria* successively carried more and more vehicles each year and she rapidly became a huge commercial success. Although the realisation of that success had been held up by the war years, it was sadly to be short lived.

Leaving Stranraer at 0745 hours on Saturday 31st January 1953, under the command of Captain James Ferguson, she set out down Loch Ryan into a full gale and driving sleet. At 0946 hours she sent the message "Hove-to off mouth of Loch Ryan. Vessel not under control. Urgent assistance of tug required". At 1032 hours she broadcast her first SOS message, her last broadcast was heard at about 1400 hours.

Unable to turn back in the storm, she had tried to cross to the shelter of the Irish coast. Although a number of ships had set out into the storm to help her, the *Princes Victoria* foundered some 8 kilometres north-east of the Copeland Islands before help could arrive. The first rescue ship on the scene was the steam coaster *Orchy*, of William Sloan & Company's Glasgow & Bristol Channel Steamers. At 1445 hours the *Orchy*, under the command of Captain Matheison, was in sight of boats and wreckage. She was later joined by HMS *Conquest*, the Bulk Oil Steamship Company's coastal tanker *Pass of Drummochter*, and the Burns and Laird steamer *Lairdsmore*. The *Princess Victoria* had sailed with 182 souls aboard; there were only 43 survivors, all men who were strong and physically fit. Amongst the dead were the Member of Parliament for North Down, Sir Walter Smiles and the Northern Ireland Minister of Finance, Major Maynard Sinclair Sinclair. The Master also died with his ship.

The subsequent Court of Inquiry was held at Belfast. It learned that the ship's stern gates had been stove-in by a heavy sea off Corsewall Point and that the car deck had become flooded whereupon the ship had begun to list to starboard. It was concluded that the scuppers on the car deck were too small to clear the mass of accumulated water and that the stern gates had been of inadequate construction. The Inquiry paid tribute to all the rescue vessels and in particular to the Donaghadee lifeboat; it concluded "If the *Princess Victoria* had been as staunch as those who manned her, then all would have been well and the disaster averted".

The tragedy had a profound effect on the development of the roll-on roll-off ferry in the United Kingdom. Indeed it was not until 1957 that a replacement for the *Princess Victoria* was even considered, and it was 1961 before the new ship, the *Caledonian Princess*, finally arrived to take up service at Stranraer. At Dover, the *Lord Warden* had been delivered before the accident, but it was 1959 before the next unit arrived in the form of the stern-loader *Maid of Kent* (see Chapter 6).

Apart from retarding the building programme of car ferries on all routes, close attention was paid by the Board of Trade to the existing stern loaders with regard to their loading doors and vehicle deck scuppers. The Townsend ferry *Halladale* (Chapter 3) became the focus of attention during her winter refit in 1953. The Board of Trade insisted that 1.2 metre long by 0.3 metre high holes be cut into the ship's hull along the car deck. During testing in dock, water was hosed onto the deck at which point the ship took on an immediate list and water flooded in! Smaller one-way scuppers were then installed and the ship was allowed to proceed back into service. The *Lord Warden* and the train ferries also had self operating scuppers installed at that time.

Memorial at Larne to the ***Princess Victoria*** disaster (*Nick Robins*)

TABLE 2. STRANRAER TO LARNE 1872 TO 1966

Name	Built	Power	Gross tons	Comments
Princess Louise	1872	Paddle	497	Sold 1890
Princess Beatrice	1875	Paddle	556	Scrapped 1904
Princess Victoria	1890	Paddle	1096	Scrapped 1910
Princess May	1892	Paddle	1123	Sold 1914
Princess Maud	1904	Turbine	1746	Scrapped 1932
Princess Victoria	1912	Turbine	1687	Scrapped 1934
Princess Margaret	1931	Turbine	2552	Sold 1962
Princess Maud	1934	Turbine	2883	Sold 1965
Princess Victoria	1939	Diesel	2197	Mined 1940
Princess Victoria	1946	Diesel	2694	Lost 1953
Hampton Ferry	1934	Turbine	2989	Sold 1969
Caledonian Princess	1961	Turbine	3630	Sold 1982

THE SHORT SEA ROUTE

The origins of the service date from 1662 when regular communication began between the ports of Donaghadee in County Down, and Portpatrick which is on the open coast to the west of Stranraer. A steamship was introduced in 1825, the Post Office having taken over the operation back in 1790. In 1837 the Royal Navy took over with the steamships *Dasher* and *Arrow*. Improvements to the two ports were made, but a Government survey reported in 1846 that better terminals would be Larne and Cairnryan. Nevertheless, railways were finally put through to both Donaghadee and Portpatrick in 1856.

The Caledonian and the London and North Western railways operated an unsuccessful service between Portpatrick and Donaghadee in 1866 and 1867, using two ex-blockade runners from the American Civil War. A service of sorts was continued for some years by local interests. These failed, however, because the contract for the carriage of mails was at that time given to G & J Burns who already ran a regular service between Belfast and Glasgow.

In 1871 the Larne & Stranraer Steamboat Company was formed in association with the Belfast & Northern Counties and the Portpatrick railways. They ordered the iron paddle steamer *Princess Louise* from Tod & McGregor of Glasgow. The steamer commenced regular sailings on 1st July 1872 between Stranraer (not Cairnryan as recommended by the earlier Government survey) and Larne. By 1874 the mails had returned to the short sea route. Successive ships on the route are listed in Table 2.

CHAPTER 5

LANDING SHIPS TANK

In June 1940, Mr Churchill identified a need for a new breed of ship which could land tanks and personnel directly onto the beaches. By October, a prototype landing ship was already on trial. Churchill's demand for a ship which could carry 60 tanks was modified by the Director of Naval Construction to a design with a more modest but more practical capacity of only 25 tanks. The result, some eighteen months later, was the Type 1 Landing Ship Tank, commonly known as the Boxer-class. Only three ships were built, all by Harland & Wolff at Belfast: HMS *Boxer*, HMS *Bruiser* and HMS *Thruster*.

Before the first of the Boxer-class was commissioned, America entered the war and the Lend-Lease Act was agreed. Under this Act it was arranged that Type 2 series ships would be built in the United States; the Type 2 Landing Ship Tank was 100 metres long by 15 metres breadth and built of all-welded construction. They were driven by two 12 cylinder diesel engines and could maintain a speed of 10 knots. In all 115 ships were transferred to Britain, of which 110 were retained as Type 2 Landing Ships Tank, and the remaining five were adapted for specialist duties.

Much of the space beneath the main tank deck was taken up by ballast compartments. This enabled the ship's trim to be adjusted to 2 metres draught forward and 4 metres aft whilst at sea, to only one metre forward and 3 metres aft on approaching a beach landing. Unfortunately the unloaded metacentric height was higher than in a normal ship and they were very susceptible to roll even in light weather.

The war record of these Type 2s reads like naval history: Malta, Sicily, Baytown (Messina), Salerno, Anzio, and then out of the Mediterranean to Operation Overlord on the Normandy beaches. The surviving Type 2 ships were all returned to the United States after the war, except for two. These strangely found their way into the ownership of a food processing company at Ayr.

An improved version of the Type 2, the Type 3 Landing Ships Tank, was first commissioned in the spring of 1945. These ships had vastly better accommodation and were constructed both in North America and in Britain to a higher specification than the Type 2s. The ships were driven by two parallel steam reciprocating engines and twin screws, and they could manage 10 knots. They were 105 to 106 metres long and 16 to 17 metres broad, depending on where they had been built. The main function of the new class was in clearing-up operations after the war, but they saw action in the relief of Norway and Denmark and the invasion of Malaya. As time went on, the Type 3s were progressively laid up in the Clyde.

The little brothers of the Landing Ships Tank were the Landing Craft Tank and the assault craft. The Landing Craft Tank came in a range of different sizes and shapes to suit a variety of different purposes. The best known classes were the Class 3 and Class 4 Landing Craft Tank, the latter being some 57 metres long by 12 metres broad and driven by twin diesels at just over 9 knots. War losses were high and included 160 Landing Craft Personnel (Large), 9 Landing Craft Infantry (Large), 9 Landing Craft Guns, 4 Landing Craft Support

(Large), and 134 Landing Craft Tank; many of the losses were sustained on the Normandy beaches.

During the war the strategic importance of the Landing Ships and Landing Craft had been repeatedly displayed. It did not require too much imagination to visualise a commercial role for the ships. The demands on merchant shipping were accentuated in the immediate post-war years by the shortage of vessels, and the lack of materials with which to construct new ships. Nevertheless, only a couple of the old Landing Craft Tank found commercial buyers, due largely to their known weakness of construction and poor sea handling. Not so the Type 3 Landing Ships Tank, which were all nearly new (completed in 1944 and 1945) and which had not suffered the ravages and extremes of war.

The man with the greatest commercial vision was undoubtably Frank Bustard. Formerly an employee of the White Star Line and latterly an army officer who had witnessed the early trials of the Landing Ships Tank at New Brighton and at Barrow Docks, Bustard was well aware of the commercial potential of these vessels. Forsaking his life-long ambition to introduce a Freddy Laker style no-frills trans-Atlantic liner service, Bustard obtained an initial three year charter on three Landing Ships Tank after much negotiation during the summer of 1946. The charter fee was a paultry £13 per ship per day! The young James Callaghan, MP, was instrumental in arranging the charter in his capacity as Parliamentary Private Secretary to the Minister of War Transport.

Delivery of the three ships took place at Tilbury, whereupon they were each put in the hands of the local office of Harland & Wolff for a three week conversion ready for their peace time role. During their refit, the wheelhouse was raised by one deck, the separate engine rooms were interconnected, crew accommodation was improved and space was set aside for twelve passengers (vehicle drivers). New funnels and navigational aids were also fitted. Vehicles could be loaded through the bow doors onto the main (tank) deck, and access to the upper deck was via a steep internal ramp. As a concession to Bustard's yen for the White Star Line, the compulsory 'Empire' names for Government ownership were followed by sympathetic second names: the *LST 3519* became the *Empire Baltic*, the *LST 3534* became the *Empire Cedric* and the *LST 3512* became the *Empire Celtic* (see Table 3).

The first voyage of the newly formed Atlantic Steam Navigation Company (named after Bustard's trans-Atlantic liner ambitions) took place on 11th September 1946. The *Empire Baltic* left Tilbury with a cargo of lorries destined for Rotterdam - duly discharged over the beach at Waalhaven where the bow doors promptly became stuck in the sand. Michael Bustard reports in the company history (Cowsill, 1990):

Eventually, the bow doors slowly opened only to find that the bottom corners of the port door stuck in the sandy bottom of the beach. The hero of the day - a Mr Bottomley, one of the stevedores - called for a spade and jumping into the water fully clothed immediately began to shovel sand away over 1 metre below the surface of the water. Eventually the door freed itself, thanks, I suspect, more to the tipping of the ship than to his digging efforts; the bow ramp came down and the cargo of lorries was driven ashore - getting rather wet in the process. The whole operation took place in this rather desolate section of the port of Rotterdam against a skyline of heavily blitzed warehouses, and I well remember the only spectators of this historic occasion were some rather thin and hungry looking Dutch boys leaning on the handle-bars of their bicycles.

The inaugural four day trip to Rotterdam was followed by the introduction of a regular service between Tilbury and Hamburg with departures every other day; the cargo comprised vehicles for the British Army of the Rhine. The service to Hamburg was maintained until 1955 when it was transferred to Antwerp. Early casualties were the *Empire Baltic* which hit a mine in September 1949, despite following the swept channel. Happily she was able to get into Emden where repairs could be carried out. Winter ice damage to the bow doors was commonplace. A small amount of commercial traffic began to join the military cargo as time went on, but British licensing restrictions severely inhibited access of Continental commercial vehicles at home, and the then nationalised British Road Services had no interest in venturing overseas.

In September 1948 the opportunity was taken to open a service to Northern Ireland. Rejected by the mighty Mersey Docks and Harbour Board, the proprietors of the Atlantic Steam Navigation Company turned to the Ports of Preston and Larne to support their new enterprise. The *Empire Doric* and the *Empire Gaelic* were acquired for the service which was actually opened by the *Empire Cedric* and the *Empire Doric*. Initial manifests listed only a few vehicles, but Frank Bustard's faith paid off as business built up; in 1950 the *Empire Gaelic* joined the other two ships at Preston to open a new service to Belfast.

Two more Landing Ships Tank were brought into the fleet in 1955: the *Empire Cymric* and the *Empire Nordic*. The fortunes of the company were enhanced in April 1953 when the Atlantic Steam Navigation Company was acquired by the British Transport Commission and many of the shares were subtly put into the name of the national haulier British Road Services. This move brought an end to the British inhibition to allow UK commercial

***Baltic Ferry** (Nick Robins)*

vehicles to venture onto the Continent.

The success of the company was recognised by the Ministry of Transport, not only in terms of its charter fees, but also by the Ministry entrusting the management of its seven operational Landing Ships Tank to the Atlantic Steam Navigation Company (which also traded under the name of The Transport Ferry Service). All the ships wore the full company livery: black hull with narrow white waist band, and a blue arrow with a white outline on the bows, and the funnel was a distinctive blue, white and black.

With the Suez Crisis in the latter part of 1956, the remaining twelve Landing Ships Tank were taken out of reserve and also entrusted to the management of the company. Each ship was given an Empire-bird name and full company colours. The total complement of nineteen ships which were now managed for the Ministry of Transport, were sent to bases at Malta, Aden and Singapore. The *Empire Cedric*, *Empire Doric* and *Empire Gaelic* were also requisitioned. These three ships were returned to the company by 1958, but the *Empire Doric* was laid up on return, and eventually sold for demolition; the *Empire Cedric*, *Empire Celtic* and *Empire Gaelic* were also scrapped in 1959 and 1960.

During 1961 the Ministry of Transport transferred the management of the military Landing Ships Tank to the British India Steam Navigation Company. British India also maintained the troopships *Dilwara*, *Dunera* and *Nevasa* at this time, and management of the Landing Ships Tank was a logical move. The ships were duly adorned in full British India colours and given the customary buff superstructure.

Management of one of the ships, the *Empire Shearwater*, was transferred to European Ferries Limited (a subsidiary of Townsend Car Ferries) in 1958. They had a purpose built link-span constructed alongside the Eastern Arm at Dover, and inaugurated a new roll-on freight only service to Calais. The new service commenced on 10th January 1959, alas, years ahead of its time, it closed in June the same year and the ship was sent to the Medway to lay up. Blame for the failure of the service was laid, rightly or wrongly, at the door of the Customs offices on both sides of the Channel. Happily the long term charter to Townsend Car Ferries was circumvented, and she was scrapped at Ghent in 1962.

The old Landing Ships Tank, having provided sterling service, were slowly being displaced by a new generation of purpose built vehicle and passenger ferries (see Chapter 10). By 1963 only the *Empire Nordic* remained with the Atlantic Steam Navigation Company, the remainder having been scrapped. The *Empire Nordic* survived until December 1966 when she was at last retired having become too expensive to maintain.

Strangely, such were the commercial demands on the company during the rebuilding programme, that another Landing Ship Tank was brought into the fleet even before the *Empire Nordic* retired. The United States Navy *LST 1080*, built in 1943 at Ambridge in America as the *Prima County*, was towed to Smith's Dock at Middlesburgh and converted into the *Baltic Ferry* (at last company ownership allowed the Empire names to be dropped). The attraction of the new ship was that the US Navy had partially rebuilt her with completely new superstructure and new diesel engines. However, she only lasted with the company until 1968, by which time she had already become surplus to requirements, and was chartered out to British Rail who put her in service between Stranraer and Larne. She was finally sold out of the company in 1972.

Empire Nordic (*Ferry Publications Library*)

In August 1966, with five new generation vehicle and passenger ferries in operation, the company acquired at auction yet another Landing Ship Tank, the former German Navy *LSD.WS.1-66* (ex-*City of Havana*, ex-*Jose Marti*, ex-HMS *Northway*). This one had been built at Newport, Virginia in 1944 and had spent much of her life laid up. She was dispatched to Palmer's Hebburn Yard for major alterations from which she emerged in February 1967 as the *Celtic Ferry*. She was given an impressive accommodation block which gave her an enlarged gross tonnage of 5556, and the same status as the new generation ferries (the *Bardic Ferry*-class) with a capacity for 55 drivers. Placed on the new Felixstowe service to Rotterdam she was very much an interim measure and was withdrawn in 1973.

The final fling of the *Baltic Ferry* and the *Celtic Ferry* saw the end of this class of ship in commercial service in UK waters. The important part that these ships had played in developing commercial roll-on roll-off links between Britain and the Continent and between England and Northern Ireland cannot be over-emphasised. Winston Churchill should perhaps assume his place in ferry design much as Brunel has retained his in the development of the railways. It was, after all, one of Churchill's Landing Ships Tank, the *Empire Cedric* which carried the world's very first all commercial (rather than military) roll-on vehicle payload on her inaugural sailing from Preston to Larne on 21st May 1948, albeit with only seven vehicles aboard.

The much smaller Landing Craft Tank and associated vessels did not fare so well in the commercial world. A number of these ships were acquired and converted for inshore ferry and excursion work but few were successful, being replaced as new post-war tonnage became available. Three notable successes are worth documenting.

The first is the *Norris Castle*, a former Landing Craft Tank which was acquired by the Southampton, Isle of Wight and South of England Royal Mail Steam Packet Company. Built in 1942, she was sent to Thorneycrofts in 1948 for major surgery which included side access to the main deck in addition to retaining the bow doors. The *Norris Castle* served her owners well, albeit in the sheltered waters of the Southampton to Cowes route, and was only retired in 1962 when the second of the company's purpose built car and passenger ferries, the *Osborne Castle* arrived in service.

Another Landing Craft Tank, *LCT 1048* was acquired by Forth Ferries Limited in 1950 and converted in the same manner as the *Norris Castle*. Renamed *Glenfinnan* she was found to be difficult to handle on the short Forth crossing and was sold to Goanese owners after only three years service.

A happier story was that of one of the Landing Craft Guns (Medium), converted into the Thames excursion steamer *Rochester Queen* of 345 tons gross, for the General Steam Navigation Company in 1948. Following the 1955 season she was sold on to German owners who gave her the name *Hein Muck*, but returned to the Red Ensign when Commodore Shipping put her on their Channel Island services as the *Commodore Queen* in 1961. Side loading facilities were then cut into her to allow carriage of a modest number of cars on her foredeck when she became a roll-on vehicle ferry. In 1973 she ran briefly for Jersey Car Ferries Limited as the *Jersey Queen* before she was sent out to West Africa to become a survey ship.

TABLE 3. TYPE 3 LANDING SHIPS TANK UNDER COMMERCIAL MANAGEMENT

Commercial name	Tons gross	Previous names and year of change
Charles Macleod	4255	
Empire Baltic	4158	ex-LST 3519 '46
Empire Cedric	4291	ex-LST 3534 '46
Empire Celtic	4291	ex-LST 3512 '46
Empire Curlew	4273	ex-*Hunter* '56; ex-LST 3042 '47
Empire Cymric	4291	ex-*Attacker* '55; ex-LST 3010 '47
Empire Doric	4291	ex-LST 3041 '48
Empire Fulmar	4267	ex-*Trumpeter* '56; ex-LST 3524 '47
Empire Gaelic	4291	ex-LST 3507 '48
Empire Gannet	4264	ex-*Tromso* '56; ex-LST 3006 '47
Empire Grebe	4251	ex-*Fighter* '56; ex-LST 3038 '47
Empire Guillemot	4255	ex-*Walcheren* '56; ex-LST 3525 '47
Empire Gull	4251	ex-*Trouncer* '56; ex-LST 3523 '47
Empire Kittiwake	4255	ex-*Slinger* '56; ex-LST 3510 '47
Empire Nordic	4157	ex-*Charger* '55; ex-LST 3026 '46
Empire Petrel	4251	ex-*Thruster* '56; ex-LST 3520 '47
Empire Puffin	4264	ex-*Battler* '56; ex-LST 3015 '47
Empire Shearwater	4262	ex-LST 3033 '56
Empire Skua	4265	ex-*St Nazaire* '56; ex-LST 3517 '47
Empire Tern	4265	ex-*Pursuer* '56; ex-LST 3504 '47
Evan Gibb	4262	
Frederick Clover	4255	
Humfrey Gale	4255	
Maxwell Brander	4255	
Reginald Kerr	4255	
Snowden Smith	4285	

CHAPTER 6

THE DINARD AND THE LORD WARDEN

The story of the *Dinard* and the *Lord Warden* illustrates the contrast between the pre-war mail-boat and the car and passenger ferry of the 1950s and 1960s.The first passenger ships to be ordered by the newly formed Southern Railway Company were the sisters *Dinard* and *St Briac.* They were both products of William Denny's yard at Dumbarton; launched on 2nd May and 2nd June 1924 respectively, they entered service on the Southampton to St Malo service later that summer. The contract for the two ships amounted to a princely £280,340. By today's standards the ships were small, with 2292 gross tons, a length of 99 metres and breadth of 13 metres, they could nevertheless accommodate 1300 passengers. The ships had steam turbine engines which drove twin screws. Their service speed was over 19 knots and they were programmed to cross to St Malo in ten hours.

Modifications to the rudders were made at an early stage in order to overcome steering difficulties in high winds. Steel plating replaced the canvas screens around the stern of the two ships during the 1931 overhaul period, but they were otherwise unaltered whilst based at Southampton.

In 1932 the *St Briac* commenced a series of short cruises taking in destinations such as Le Havre, Rouen, Jersey, Guernsey and St Malo over a four day period. Each cruise carried an average of 165 passengers. The cruises were a great success; there were 15 in 1932 and another 22 in 1933 and 19 more in the following year. This pattern carried on throughout the thirties, with the steamer occasionally going as far as Antwerp. These were the first cruises operated by a railway ship and they gave her the unique distinction of being fitted with an open-air swimming pool.

There were two Spithead Naval Reviews at which both ships were present, the first on 16th July 1935 to celebrate the Silver Jubilee of King George V, and the second on 20th May 1937 in honour of the Coronation of King George VI. Other members of the Southampton railway fleet were also present: the *Isle of Sark, Brittany, Normannia* and *Isle of Guernsey* at both Reviews and the *Isle of Jersey* in addition at the 1937 Review.

The *Isle of Sark*, built in 1932, carried two engineering distinctions. She was the first British ship to be built with a Maierform bow, which was claimed to reduce water resistance in calm seas and to improve handling in rough weather. The second distinction was the more important: at the invitation of her builders, William Denny, an offer was made to equip the ship with the new Denny-Brown stabiliser for £6,400, with half of the cost to be borne by Denny if the experiment was unsuccessful and only a third if successful. As we now know, the experiment was a great success.

On 2nd October 1939 the *Dinard* was requisitioned for use as a hospital ship, initially based at Newhaven. The *St Briac* remained on Southampton to Le Havre, St Malo and Channel Isles duties, the Le Havre service terminating on 19th May 1940 due to the advancing German army. The last mail-boat contact before the occupation of the Channel Islands was on 29th June when the *Isle of Sark* left Guernsey with 647 passengers for

Lord Warden *(Nick Robins)*

Southampton.

The *St Briac* was moved to the Bristol Channel as a personnel ship. In September 1941 she became a navigational practice target for the Royal Naval Air Station at Arbroath. On 12th March the next year she struck two mines within twenty minutes of each other, broke her back and sank with the loss of 43 lives. In the mean time, the *Dinard*, still a hospital ship, moved north to Scapa Flow. In June 1944 the *Dinard* took part in the Normandy Landings, returning the wounded to England. On 7th June she hit a mine while off "Juno Beach" and was beached for temporary repairs before returning to Southampton and dry dock.

At the close of hostilities the *Dinard* was returned to the Southern Railway Company. On 9th August 1946 she left Southampton on commercial service for the last time, almost 22 years after her maiden voyage from that same port. She was sent to Palmer's Hebburn yard for radical alteration. The Southern Railway Company had decided that the little *Autocarrier* (Chapter 3) was no longer adequate to support the anticipated post-war demand for car and passenger traffic out of Dover and had identified the elderly *Dinard* as her replacement.

Her accommodation was totally rebuilt and her new passenger complement became a mere 300. A garage for 80 cars was cut into the after third section of the main deck, with loading gates provided at the stern; gross tonnage was reduced to 1769. On 1st July 1947 the newly converted *Dinard* inaugurated a new summer only car ferry service between Dover and Boulogne, Calais for the moment loosing its railway company car ferry service. For the next six years the service depended on crane loading at Dover, although drive on facilities were introduced in 1952 at Boulogne. Meanwhile, drive on facilities had become available at Calais, thanks to the efforts of Townsend Car Ferries, in 1951.

The railway and shipping services of all the railway companies suffered badly during the war. In an attempt to redress lack of efficiency and organisation, the railways were nationalised with effect from 1st January 1948. This had the immediate effect of placing all the railway ships under the single banner of the British Transport Commission. The shipping services were managed on a regional basis, the services out of Dover falling under the jurisdiction of the Southern Region.

So successful was the converted *Dinard* on the Boulogne service that immediate consideration was given to the building of a new drive-on drive-off ferry for the route. The British Transport Commission had inherited one purpose built car and passenger ferry, the ill-fated *Princess Victoria* (Chapter 4), but there was also considerable experience with the operation of roll-on roll-off services provided by the Dover and Harwich train ferries.

The construction of the new ship was again entrusted to Denny. The ship was given the name *Lord Warden* (the third Dover ship to carry the name) and was launched on 14th November 1951 by Mrs John Elliot. The *Lord Warden* had a gross tonnage of 3333, was 110 metres long by 18 metres breadth. She was driven by oil fired steam turbine engines and twin screws which gave her a service speed of 20 knots, and she was equipped with a bow rudder and stabilizers.

She had accommodation for 770 passengers, exceptionally 1000 at peak times, and 120 cars. Access to the car deck was via a recessed open deck (at belting level) protected from the sea by low hinged gates in a similar manner to the arrangement in use on the *Princess Victoria* at Stranraer and on the train ferries. The main accommodation was on "B" deck, one up from the car deck, and included a lounge, tea bar, waitress service restaurant, a gift shop and a bank, the RAC and AA offices, a passport office and the purser. There were also seven private cabins. "A" Deck was the promenade or boat deck which contained the smoke room bar forward.

The maiden commercial voyage of the *Lord Warden* was on 16th June 1952 under the command of Captain Gordon Walker. Radio messages were exchanged during the voyage with the then Lord Warden, Sir Winston Churchill. The new ship rapidly developed an unprecedented popularity with the travelling public, many travellers designing their journeys around the schedules of the *Lord Warden* rather than travel on the *Dinard.* Nevertheless, the new Boulogne car ferry service went from strength to strength, with support, rather than competition from Townsend's *Halladale* on the Calais service.

The *Lord Warden* was in every way an innovative land mark in cross Channel ferry design. She takes her place alongside the first *Princess Victoria* and the Townsend ferry *Forde*; the development of the modern vehicle ferry owes a great deal to all three ships and to their marine architects. It was fitting that the *Lord Warden* should be shown off by her owners when less than a year old at the Coronation Naval Review of 1953, very much following in the steps of her elder consort the *Dinard.*

The *Lord Warden* received a fireman's helmet to her funnel in 1956. This was required in order to cure the hitherto unpleasant down-draught of fumes from the original funnel arrangement. In 1978 the funnel height was increased and the helmet became partially

Maid of Kent (Nick Robins)

concealed. This work was undertaken just prior to the transfer of the vessel to the Irish Sea.

At the end of the 1978 season the stern half-gates were replaced (they really stemmed from another era by then). Two new gates were installed which at last protected the vehicle deck right up to the poop or "B" deck level. It will be recalled that it was the stoving-in of half gates that was instrumental in the loss of the *Princess Victoria* in 1953. A cross-wise girder was also fixed across the stern to lock the upper part of the gates. This prohibited the carriage of high vehicles which had previously been accommodated in the well aft of the "B" deck housing.

During the 1964/65 winter the ship became one of the first to wear the new company colours. She received the attractive dark blue-green hull and was given the red funnel with twin arrow device in place of the familiar buff with black top. The upperworks were at one time painted pale blue but these quickly reverted to white with a touch of blue-grey.

The elderly *Dinard* plodded on alongside the *Lord Warden*. She was not used as intensely as the new ship and she was able to spend much of the winter period out of service. Nevertheless, she became an increasingly expensive unit to operate and was finally withdrawn from service in October 1958. Amazingly, at the age of 35, she was sold for further service in Finland with many years of active service ahead of her.

The replacement of the *Dinard* for the 1959 season was the magnificent *Maid of Kent*, the "pocket liner". The *Maid of Kent* was the first stern-loading car ferry to be designed and built with full cognisance of the conclusions of the *Princess Victoria* Inquiry. She was the first British car ferry to be built with a hydraulic stern door which was hinged in the horizontal plain so that it could be lowered raised out of the way during loading. The stern door was designed to be completely water-tight so that it formed an integral part of the hull of the ship. Like the *Lord Warden*, the *Maid of Kent* was also powered by steam turbine engines. The *Maid of Kent* was finally withdrawn in 1981 and sold for demolition in northern Spain.

Five further passenger and car ferries were built with steam turbine propulsion (Table 4). This system of power was attractive in a passenger ship because it was almost vibration free. Its attraction diminished throughout the 1960s because it became less and less economical when compared with the increasingly efficient marine diesel. Rising fuel costs in the 1970s eventually put the steam turbine out of business.

Three of the five new turbine ships were for railway service, the *Caledonian Princess* for Stranraer, as the replacement for the *Princess Victoria*, the *Dover* for the burgeoning Dover to Boulogne service, and the *Holyhead Ferry I* to open a new car ferry service between Holyhead and Dun Laoghaire alongside the mailships *Hibernia* and *Cambria*, but as a direct replacement for the elderly *Princess Maud*.

In retrospect it is interesting to note that the London, Midland & Scottish Railway Company were happy with diesel for the pre-war *Princess Victoria* and her post-war replacement, but the more conservative Government controlled British Transport Commission reverted to more traditional motive power. The only other organisation to stick doggedly with the steam turbine were the equally conservative Directors of the Isle of Man Steam Packet Company (the *Manx Maid* and *Ben-my-Chree*, see Chapter 9).

As for the *Lord Warden*, she continued in service mainly in the Irish Sea in her later years, until 1979 when she was laid up at Milford Haven. She later saw service under the Saudi Arabian flag as the *Al Zaher*, as such her new stern gates were supplemented with the addition of a stern ramp. In 1981 she finally arrived at Gadani Beach in Pakistan for breaking up.

TABLE 4. PURPOSE-BUILT STEAM TURBINE PASSENGER AND CAR FERRIES

Name	Built	Gross tons	Number of passengers	Number of cars
Lord Warden	1952	3333	770/1000	120
Maid of Kent	1959	3920	1000	190
Caledonian Princess	1961	3629	1400	80
Holyhead Ferry I	1965	3879	1000	160
Dover	1965	3602	1000	160
*Manx Maid**	1962	2725	1400	90
*Ben-my-Chree**	1966	2762	1400	90

* Side-loaders - Isle of Man Steam Packet Company (Chapter 9)

CHAPTER 7

THE FREE ENTERPRISE CLASS

The blossoming of Townsend Ferries 'Free Enterprise' fleet is noteworthy on three counts. Firstly, the design of the first of the new ships, the *Free Enterprise*, produced a passenger and car ferry rather than a passenger ferry which could take cars. Secondly, the *Free Enterprise II* was the first British drive-through ferry. Thirdly, the tremendously successful *Free Enterprise IV*-class of ships (five in all) illustrates the long anticipated explosion in freight traffic and the steady increase in the demand for accompanied cars from the late 1960s onwards.

Innovative although all eight Free Enterprise ships were, it is necessary to put that innovation into an international perspective. Way back in 1939, Mr Stuart Townsend had visited Norway with a view to purchasing the Fredrikshavn to Larvik ferry *Peter Wessel*. This ship was 25 years ahead of any British counterpart in design, as she incorporated a car deck with headroom sufficient to accommodate the lorries of the day and a bow loading door which provided drive-through facilities. The first British ship to match the *Peter Wessel* was the *Free Enterprise III*, but she was only introduced into service in 1966.

The *Free Enterprise* was designed and built as a replacement for the *Halladale* (Chapter 3). The responsibility for the design of the new ship was given by George Nott to a young naval architect, Mr James Ayres, formerly of Norman Dewar. James Ayres' ideas contrasted sharply with those of the traditional designs of the British Transport Commission, not least in his preference for diesel engines. Far more radical were such features as twin funnels, open-plan lounges and a vehicle deck which had a headroom of nearly 5 metres in anticipation of an uptake in freight traffic.

The annual refits of the *Halladale* in Amsterdam had provided an introduction to the shipbuilding company Werf Gusto at Schiedam. It was this yard that was to build all the Free Enterprise ships except the *Free Enterprise VIII*, the latter contract being awarded to the same company but built at their Verolme Shipyard at Alblasserdam. James Ayres, however, was the designer of all of the ships in the Free Enterprise class, later becoming the company's Technical Director.

The *Free Enterprise* was equipped with two 12 cylinder diesel engines driving twin screws. She had a service speed of nearly 19 knots, and feathering propellers gave direct control of the speed of the vessel to the bridge. She had a bow rudder, a modestly powered bow thrust unit with electric drive, Decca navigation aids and conventional long range radar.

The new ship entered service on 22nd April 1962. Built at a cost of £1 million, she was launched on 2nd February 1962 having only been eight months on the slipway. She had a gross tonnage of 2607 and was 96 metres in length. She was much stubbier than anything seen before, with a breadth of 16 metres. Accommodation was provided for 120 cars on two decks, but the middle section of the main car deck was able to take about eight large and high vehicles in two or three lanes depending on vehicle width. A hinged ramp came down from the roof of the main car deck to give access to the shelter deck garage. At the after end of the main car deck was a large turntable which enabled coaches and other large vehicles to be turned on boarding, and backed up the ship in readiness for disembarkation.

In the first twelve months operation of the *Free Enterprise*, 83500 cars and a quarter of a million passengers were carried between Dover and Calais. This compared most favourably with the 27500 cars carried in the final year of service of the old *Halladale*. During 1964 the ship adopted the new name *Free Enterprise I*.

On 29th January 1965 the next ship, the *Free Enterprise II*, was launched at Schiedam. She was the very first British drive-through ferry. This ship was also by far the largest British car ferry to date, measuring some 4122 tons gross with a length of 108 metres and a breadth of 18 metres. The ship cost £1.3 million to build.

The *Free Enterprise II* was not provided with the same headroom clearance on the car deck as the *Free Enterprise I*, because the demand for freight traffic had still not materialised. Nevertheless she could accommodate 1200 passengers and 200 cars. She was one of the first British ferries to be equipped with the flume stabilizer system - only partially successful, and dropped in subsequent years in favour of the fin stabilizer. Nevertheless the *Free Enterprise II* represented the state-of-the-art (described in the press at the time as the last word in ferry design) as she undertook her maiden voyage on 22nd May 1965.

Within her first year of service the *Free Enterprise II* inaugurated a new service between Dover and Zeebrugge. It was on this route that the demand for the carriage of lorries was finally realised. Sadly the *Free Enterprise II* was quickly outmoded because of the restricted headroom on her vehicle deck, and she was relegated to a seasonal car and passenger ferry at a very tender age. The ship was, however, adapted for twin level loading at Dover once this facility became available at her home port. She should not be forgotten though, as the *Free Enterprise II* represents the first stern and bow loader to fly the red ensign, and she remains very much a credit to her designer.

A near sister was the next ship of the fleet, the *Free Enterprise III*. Launched on 14th May 1966, this ship had taken less than six months to build at a cost of £2 million. Unlike the *Free Enterprise II*, the car decks were arranged on three levels, a Well Deck with a headroom of 2.5 metres and the Mezzanine Deck and Shelter Deck each with a headroom of nearly 3 metres, but outside the exhaust uptakes were the two Main Decks which had a clearance of 4 metres, and were used for freight vehicles. In all, 14 lorries could be carried on the Main Deck plus 100 cars, or in the absence of any lorries she could take 220 cars. Two level loading was adopted at Dover over the stern of the ship. She could carry 1200 passengers.

The ship was to witness a tremendous growth in freight traffic with ever larger vehicles forced into the two single lane alleyways on the Main Deck. Freight traffic amounted to just under 2700 vehicles on the Calais and Zeebrugge services in 1966, but in 1967 it had increased to 17250, of which 75% of the increase was credited to the Zeebrugge service. Resort was often made aboard the new *Free Enterprise III*, to the use of soapy water in order to slip trailer wheels round the kerbs protecting the exhaust uptakes, but during overhaul periods the *Free Enterprise II* found it increasingly hard to cope with the freight traffic.

The freight build up continued on the Zeebrugge service. The company was restricted in growth at Zeebrugge by its tenure of a small corner of the Baudouin Canal, and pressure was brought to bear on the Belgians to provide better facilities even though this service was in direct competition with their own State owned Ostend service. As an interim measure the freighter *Autocarrier* joined the fleet (see Chapter 8) until a new series of ferries was introduced with the

Free Enterprise I (Nick Robins)

Free Enterprise II (FotoFlite)

launch of the *Free Enterprise IV* on 1st March 1969. The *Free Enterprise IV* entered service on 1st June on the Zeebrugge service and became the first vessel alongside the new Zeebrugge berth when it was opened in April 1972.

The new *Free Enterprise IV*-class of ship had a gross tonnage of just over 5000 and measured some 117 metres long by 20 metres breadth. There were five ships all built to the same basic design, culminating in the *Free Enterprise VIII* which undertook her maiden voyage on 18th July 1974. This class of ship is all the more remarkable in that all the ships were built during a period of complete stagnation in the development of the rival British Rail fleet; the Government owned ferry operation was fearful, even then, that any investment could be overtaken by the Channel Tunnel.

The five ships each differed in a number of subtle ways. The first two were equipped with Smit MAN engines whereas the last three had Stork-Werkspoor engines; flume stabilizers were dropped for the last three ships in favour of fin stabilizers. Basically, however, all the ships had accommodation for 1125 passengers and 220 cars except the *Free Enterprise VIII* which had a slightly larger capacity for 275 cars and was in any case some 6 metres longer than her sisters.

The Free Enterprise fleet led a largely uneventful life and enjoyed the boom years of the developing car and freight trade very much at the expense of the state owned railway services. There were occasional press reports of incidents such as problems with road tankers full of chemicals, and temporary withdrawals to sort belting out after striking berths too hard in adverse weather. But by far the worst incident was the engine room explosion which the *Free Enterprise III* suffered whilst 35 kilometres off Cherbourg in July 1970.

In 1968, George Nott bought out and merged Townsend Ferries with the Norwegian owned

Free Enterprise at the Eastern Docks (*FotoFlite*)

Thoresen Ferries which had operated out of Southampton to France since 1964, so creating the European Ferries' Townsend Thoresen empire. The amalgamation of the respective services provided considerable flexibility for the operation of the combined fleets. Indeed, it was the seasonal car ferry services to Cherbourg that provided the *Free Enterprise II* with a new niche.

The Atlantic Steam Navigation Company (Chapter 5) was acquired by the Group in November 1971 for £5.5 million. Shortly afterwards the opportunity was taken to move their Irish Sea services from Preston to Cairnryan, so providing a more efficient use of the ships with a much reduced passage time. The *Free Enterprise III* was transferred to this new service for an experimental summer season starting in July 1974. The following year the new service was operated by the *Free Enterprise I*, and in 1976 the *Free Enterprise IV* went north and was so successful that she remained there on a year round basis for the next ten years.

Seasonal weekend sailings were introduced between Dover and Boulogne in 1973, usually with the *Free Enterprise VI.* In subsequent years it was common to find the oldest three units of the fleet laid up at Tilbury during the winter months. The *Free Enterprise I* was the first of the ships to be sold out of the fleet at the age of eighteen - she went for further service with Greek owners. The *Free Enterprise II* was sold during 1982 to Sardinian owners.

The *Free Enterprise III* was disposed of in July 1984 to the Mira Shipping Line of Malta and renamed the *Tamira.* Amazingly, by October, she had returned to Britain bearing the name *Mona's Isle*, following a £600,000 deal with the Isle of Man Steam Packet Company. From then on her copy book was not just blotted but thoroughly screwed up. Conversion by her new owners limited the ship to a commercial vehicle payload of only 200 tonnes. To make matters worse she managed to miss the harbour entrance at Heysham on one occasion and was lucky not

***Free Enterprise VII** (Nick Robins)*

to end up beached as a permanent feature beneath the leisure centre at Half Moon Bay. In due course the Steam Packet Board of Directors announced that she would be put up for disposal.

The success of the five ships of the *Free Enterprise IV*-class is legion. Indeed two of these ships survive to this day, albeit in jumboised form, in the fleet of P&O European Ferries on the Cairnryan service. Although the *Free Enterprise IV* was sold to the Greek registry in 1988, the remaining four ships were given Pride of... names by P&O following takeover of the Townsend Thoresen Group in December 1986. The desirability of a new livery and new names had been hastened by the loss of the *Herald of Free Enterprise* in March of the following year (Chapter 14).

The impact made by James Ayres and the 'Free Enterprise' ships cannot be over estimated. Coincident with a boom in car and freight demand, all eight ships were entirely right for the day, save perhaps for the *Free Enterprise II* with her inadequate vehicle deck headroom.

Towards the end of the Dover to Boulogne service, two tired ships clearly showed their vintage as the *Free Enterprise V* and *Free Enterprise VIII* masqueraded under the dark blue liveries of P&O with the respective names of *Pride of Hythe* and *Pride of Canterbury*. They were almost time pieces from another age - attractive wood panelling, small of scale and generally insufficient for the demands of the 1990s, but following the closure of the Dover-Boulogne service the pair were sold to a Cypriot and a Greek company respectively in 1993. By contrast, the jumboized *Pride of Rathlin* (ex-*Pride of Walmer*, ex-*Free Enterprise VII*) and her sister *Pride of Ailsa* (formerly the *Pride of Sandwich*, ex-*Free Enterprise VI*), now transferred to the Larne service, had managed to attain the trappings expected of the traveller in the 1990s. These are adaptable ships indeed.

Pride of Canterbury *(Miles Cowsill)*

Free Enterprise IV (Ferry Publications Library)

CHAPTER 8

CONVERSIONS

During the 1960s, all the major British-flag passenger ferry operators found themselves with an embarrassing shortage of roll-on roll-off vessels. The British Transport Commission, Coast Lines Seaway and even the Caledonian Steam Packet Company, for example, had invested heavily in the 1950s, but mainly in passenger-only ships. The time had come when there were just not enough car ferries available for the business on offer. The under capacity was due to both the traditional resistance of the larger companies to the new drive-on concept, and to the aftermath of the *Princess Victoria* disaster (Chapter 4).

The British Transport Commission had built some car ferries (Chapter 6), but these were not enough. Coast Lines and its associate companies were still building the same basic Harland & Wolff-type *Ulster Monarch*-class of passenger ship dating from 1929, right up until the *Scottish Coast* was completed in 1957 (built by the mile, cut off by the yard!). In Scotland, the Caledonian Steam Packet Company had put the magnificent *Glen Sannox* in operation between Ardrossan and Brodick back in 1957, following the successful introduction of the "ABC" class to the Clyde in 1953 (Chapter 13). Nevertheless, a shortage of car capacity was to manifest itself even here by the late 1960s.

Meanwhile, of course, Townsend Car Ferries and the Atlantic Steam Navigation Company thought only of roll-on roll-off traffic. These two companies, coupled with the Norwegian-flag Thoresen Ferries, which started operating out of Southampton in 1964, and other foreign-flag car ferry services to Britain, posed a very significant threat to the well-being of the traditional carriers.

The first reaction from the British Railways Board was on the Fishguard to Rosslare service. This route had been maintained for many years by the pre-war *St Andrew* and the 1947 built *St David.* At the end of the 1963 season, the younger ship was withdrawn from service and converted into a side-loading car and passenger ferry (Table 5). Outwardly, the ship was not greatly changed in appearance, but clearance of much of the cabin accommodation inside the ship made way for the new garage. The success of the conversion was demonstrated by the annual carriage of cars on the route: only 11,000 in 1963 but 20,000 in 1964.

The withdrawal of the Southampton to Le Havre and Southampton to St Malo services of British Railways led to the release of the passenger steamers *Normannia* and *Falaise.* The *Normannia* was sent to Hawthorn Leslie's yard on the Tyne in 1964, where she was converted into a stern-loading car ferry with accommodation for 500 passengers (formerly 1400 passengers) and 111 cars. On 21st April 1964 she took up service as a car ferry under Captain Elgar Blaxland on the Dover to Boulogne service alongside the *Lord Warden* and the *Maid of Kent.* She survived in this guise until 1979, although she was briefly registered at Calais under the ownership of SNCF during part of 1973.

The *Falaise* was sent to the Vickers Armstrong Yard at Hebburn on the Tyne for similar treatment. She emerged with a capacity of 700 passengers and 100 cars (as a passenger only ferry she used to carry 1400 passengers). She was immediately placed on the new car ferry service between Newhaven and Dieppe which she opened on 1st June 1964. She was joined by two new

***Falaise** (Nick Robins)*

French ferries, the *Villandry* and *Valencay* in 1965, each with accommodation for 1200 passengers and 140 cars. The partnership was broken with the arrival of the new *Senlac* in 1973; the *Falaise* transferred to Weymouth only to be sold for demolition in Spain two years later. The conversion of both the *Falaise* and the *Normannia* was completed within a budget, granted by the Minister of Transport, of only £700,000.

Rumour that the long-standing Heysham to Belfast night ferry service was to be abandoned was rife during the winter months 1964/65. This service was operated by three passenger only ships which had hold space for crane-loaded cars, railway containers and live cattle. At any one time, two ships maintained the service and the third was on stand-by or at overhaul, except when the *Duke of Lancaster* was away cruising, particularly around the Scottish islands. An atmosphere of inevitable redundancy hung over the service in the spring of 1964, when in May, the British Railways Board unexpectedly announced that two of the ships would be converted into stern-loading car and passenger ferries and retained at Heysham.

The two ships were the *Duke of Argyll* and the *Duke of Lancaster*. One by one, they were returned to their builder, Harland & Wolff at Belfast, so that "D" Deck could be stripped out to become the car deck, and the new stern access doors installed. At the same time the ships were converted to single class accommodation which enabled enlargement of some of the public rooms.

The new car and passenger service was initially a great success, but it was soon to lose traffic to the Atlantic Steam Navigation Company at Cairnryan. Seasonal day time services were introduced, mainly at weekends, in order to attract new business. Regrettably, at the age of 70, the loss-making Heysham to Belfast link finally closed on 1st February 1975. The *Duke of Argyll* was sold for further service in the Mediterranean, but the *Duke of Lancaster* moved to Holyhead

Duke of Rothesay *(Nick Robins)*

to displace her former running mate, the *Duke of Rothesay.* The *Duke of Lancaster* was eventually sold in 1979.

The *Duke of Rothesay* had maintained the Heysham service whilst her two sisters were being converted. In 1966 she had become surplus to requirements and was herself converted into a side-loading car ferry to run alongside the *St David* at Fishguard. The arrival of the *Duke of Rothesay* allowed the pre-war *St Andrew* to retire. The *Duke of Rothesay* arrived on station in May 1967. She remained at Fishguard until she also was displaced, this time by another convert, the *Avalon,* formerly of the Harwich to Hook service. The *Duke of Rothesay* was sold for demolition at Faslane in 1975.

The *Avalon* was built for £2 million by Alexander Stephen & Sons in 1963 as the flagship of the British Railways fleet. She was very well appointed and was frequently used for cruising, both around Britain and to European destinations. However, she too had a stern gate cut into her and cabin accommodation stripped out in order to garage 210 cars. Her passenger complement was 1200, with new accommodation constructed over the poop deck. The work was carried out by Swan Hunter on the Tyne for a total cost of £1 million.

The car ferry *Avalon* was used both at Fishguard and at Holyhead. Throughout, she managed to retain the air of a flagship and she developed her own following amongst the travelling public. Alas, she too was withdrawn in September 1980. It is questionable that a passenger only ship, and one with steam turbine engines, should ever have been built for the Harwich service as late as 1963; in her original form she was a handsome ship, but one that was built for another era, bearing in mind that the order was placed for the first car ferry for the route only three years later. Sadly, the seventeen year old ship was sold for scrap in Pakistan, adopting the name *Valon* for the delivery voyage.

The way in which the Coast Lines Seaway coped with the problem of inadequate car capacity took three routes: do nothing, convert for car carrying, or newbuilding. None of these routes proved entirely satisfactory. The first line of action, or rather inaction, hastened the withdrawal, in October 1967, of the traditional overnight Glasgow to Belfast ferries the *Royal Scotsman* (registered in Glasgow) and the *Royal Ulsterman* (registered, of course, in Belfast). Three sailings per week were subsequently maintained by the *Irish Coast* until 1968, and then by the *Scottish Coast*; the service terminating on 30th August 1969. The direct sailing between Glasgow and Dublin had already ceased.

A more critical need for car capacity was that of the daylight route between Ardrossan and Belfast, so the *Scottish Coast* was put on this service between 1965 and 1967 as an interim measure prior to the arrival of newbuilding (Chapter 9). Before starting on the Ardrossan service she was converted to car carrying with the addition of a massive and ungainly lift structure which was erected on the fore-deck and which enabled cars to be driven off the quay onto the lift and so down to the forward hold. Turntables were strategically placed to help stow the cars, and a fire sprinkler system was installed. With this arrangement the new "car ferry" could accommodate between 20 and 25 cars, but no freight vehicles.

During this same era there were a number of notable conversions of passenger ship to car or freight ferry. The magnificent, but rather heavy-on-fuel, fast day-ferry the *Brighton* retired from the British Railways Newhaven to Dieppe service in 1967 and passed into the ownership of Jersey Line. Renamed the *La Duchesse de Bretagne*, provision was made for the carriage of 25 cars with drive-on access provided by ship-board ramps hinged off the after-deck. Services were maintained from Torquay, Plymouth, Weymouth, Poole and Southampton to Jersey, Guernsey, St Malo and Cherbourg, but they were not a success and the ship was withdrawn after the 1968 season.

La Duchesse de Bretagne (Nick Robins)

Duke of Argyll *(Nick Robins)*

Perhaps the most dramatic conversion was the rebuilding of the Thames excursion ship *Royal Sovereign* into the Townsend Car Ferries freight carrier *Autocarrier*. The *Royal Sovereign* was completed in 1948 by William Denny (Dumbarton) and was one of three excursion ships operated by the General Steam Navigation Company until the end of the 1966 summer season. Townsend Ferries bought her for £100,000 and spent a further £150,000 on her conversion. In her new form she could accommodate 24 lorries and had a much reduced passenger certificate for 36. She started work on the Dover to Zeebrugge route on 30th August 1967; she was later sold for further service under the Italian flag in 1973.

Passenger to car ferry conversions also took place in the Clyde fleet of the Caledonian Steam Packet Company. Here the hugely successful hoist-loading ferries the *Glen Sannox*, *Arran*, *Bute* and *Cowal* (the *Glen Sannox* and *Arran* were later converted to stern loaders in 1969 and 1973 respectively) had demonstrated the value of car ferries, and had developed the market for the carriage of cars. As a precursor to new tonnage, the passenger only *Maid of Cumbrae*, dating from 1953, was given stern and side ramps and the after part of her deck accommodation was cut away to allow room for 15 cars. She re-entered service in May 1972, between Gourock and Dunoon, but was displaced to spare ship at the end of 1974 and was eventually sold in 1978. Her three sisters were not converted, and they became redundant during 1973 and 1974.

Three new side-loaders had been delivered in 1964 into what was to become the Caledonian MacBrayne fleet (Chapter 13). One of these, the *Clansman* was lengthened by 12 metres during the winter of 1972/73, and at the same time converted into a drive-through car ferry with bow and stern loading. (Examples of jumboisation, rather than conversion, are given in Chapter 15). The *Clansman* was placed on the Ardrossan to Brodick service where she was able to maintain a very successful second career. She was sold in 1984.

Autocarrier *(Nick Robins)*

Conversions in some form or other have continued to this day. The stern loaders *Holyhead Ferry I* and *Dover* (see Table 4, Chapter 6) were converted to drive-through ships in 1976/77, albeit with reduced passenger certificates, and renamed *Earl Leofric* and *Earl Siward* respectively.

In more recent years, conversion of freight ferry to vehicle and passenger ferry has been successfully carried out in a number of cases. Examples from the 1980's include provision for the former *Baltic Ferry* and *Nordic Ferry* (on the Townsend Thoresen Felixstowe to Zeebrugge service, now respectively the *Pride of Suffolk* and *Pride of Flanders* under P&O European Ferries) to carry 650 passengers (vice 166 lorry drivers), and the conversion of the Sealink freighter *Darnia* (ex-*Stena Topper*) to carry up to 412 passengers.

TABLE 5. BRITISH RAILWAYS STEAM TURBINE PASSENGER FERRIES CONVERTED TO CAR AND PASSENGER FERRIES

Name	Period as passenger ferry	Length (m)	Breadth (m)	Original gross tons	Period as car ferry	New Gross tons
Avalon	1963-1975	123	18	6584	1975-1980	6707
Duke of Argyll	1956-1964	115	17	4797	1964-1975	4450
Duke of Lancaster	1956-1964	115	17	4797	1964-1979	4450
Duke of Rothesay*	1957-1966	115	17	4780	1966-1975	4138
Falaise	1947-1964	95	15	3710	1964-1975	2416
Normannia	1952-1964	94	15	3543	1964-1979	2219
St David*	1947-1963	98	15	3352	1963-1970	3783

* Side loaders

CHAPTER 9

FIRST GENERATION CAR FERRIES

As Townsend Car Ferries and the Atlantic Steam Navigation Company led a reluctant British Railways Board into the car ferry era, a flush of first generation car ferries were being built for a variety of routes around our shores.

On the Irish Sea, Coast Lines Seaway, in the form of the British and Irish Steam Packet Company, put the drive-through car ferries *Munster* and *Innisfallen*, with their distinctive witches hat funnels, into service in 1968. The *Innisfallen* was bought on the stocks at Rendsburg; designed for service in the Baltic she actually had a hull strengthened for contact with ice. The *Munster* was built in Hamburg and a third ship, the *Leinster* was built at home in Cork. These three Irish-flag ferries maintained the Liverpool to Dublin and the new Swansea to Cork services. For the latter service, the *Innisfallen* had an exceptionally fast service speed of 24 knots.

Further north, two most handsome car ferries were commissioned in the spring of 1967 for the overnight Liverpool to Belfast service of the Belfast Steamship Company. The *Ulster Prince* came from Harland & Wolff at Belfast, and the *Ulster Queen* was built by Cammell Laird, just across the water from the Princes Dock Terminal at Liverpool. They were driven by 12 cylinder vee-type Crossley Pielstick oil engines and had a service speed of just over 17 knots. The sisters had a gross tonnage of 4479, and could accommodate 1022 passengers and 140 cars.

In 1976, the Coast Lines Group was taken over by P&O. Nevertheless, the two Belfast boats did not survive much longer, and in December 1981, the two ships sailed for lay-up at Ostend, the *Ulster Queen* going eventually to Greek owners and the *Ulster Prince* to the Cypriot flag. There had been many problems with the design of the two ships. They were, for example, two class ships and, therefore, required extra catering staff; the total crew complement was 85. They were stern-loaders with a restricted headroom at the stern door of only 4.1 metres, even though part of the vehicle deck had a free height of 4.9 metres. The vehicle deck was further limited by the retention of a conventional hold space forward. By 1979, and again in 1980 they were loosing over £0.5 million a year, and this coupled with crew strikes during 1981, made closure of the service inevitable.

Another wing of the Coast Lines empire, Burns & Laird, received one new car ferry, the *Lion*, from Cammell Laird also in 1967. She started on the Ardrossan to Belfast service on a stormy 3rd January 1968, adopting a 1000 hours departure from Ardrossan and a leisurely 1630 hours return after the 270 minute crossing. Unlike the Liverpool ships, the *Lion* was designed as a drive-through ship with space for 140 cars and a hinged mezzanine deck which left room for up to 40 lorries with a height of 4.4 metres. Her design, though still only of a first generation car ferry, was much more far seeing than that of her two counterparts at Liverpool. The ship was of 3333 tons gross and she could carry 1200 passengers. At the time of the P&O take-over, the service closed in the face of severe competition from the Stranraer and Cairnryan to Larne services, and the ship was transferred to her new owner's Dover to Boulogne route. She stayed there until sold to Cypriot owners in 1985, but served on charter as the Channel Islands Ferries *Portelet* for the 1987 and 1988 seasons.

Lion *(Nick Robins)*

Manx Maid *(Nick Robins)*

No attempt was made to bring the roll-on roll-off concept to the northernmost arm of Coast Lines, the North of Scotland, Orkney & Shetland service, for many years. Indeed the conventional passenger and cargo ferry *St Clair* had only been introduced in 1960, and was eventually replaced in 1977 by surplus tonnage from the P&O Group fleet on the South Coast (the *SF Panther*, see below) which was only three years her junior.

Another traditional passenger ferry operator is the Isle of Man Steam Packet Company. The response of this company to the car ferry era was quite unique. It comprised a car and passenger ferry which was based on a well tried and tested design of passenger only ship (the *Manxman* and her forebears) and which included a spiral set of ramps at the stern. The spiral connected the car deck with the quay at any stage of the tide, even at Douglas where there is a 7 metre tidal range. There was a turntable at the forward end of the Main Deck garage. At the stern the spiral roadway makes five turns, three aft and two forward, to provide access to loading ports on the Shelter Deck and the Promenade Deck. The system avoided the need for hinged linkspans at the many company terminals (Liverpool, Douglas, Ardrossan, Belfast, Dublin etc).

Four such car ferries were built. The first was the *Manx Maid*, which was completed by Cammell Laird in 1962 at a cost of £1.1 million. She had a gross tonnage of 2724 and was 99 metres long by 15 metres broad. She was equipped with two Pametrada steam turbine engines which gave her a service speed of 21 knots, and she was the first ship in the fleet with stabilizers. There was accommodation for 1400 passengers and 90 cars; the crew complement was 60. Her maiden voyage took place between Liverpool and Douglas under the command of Captain J E Quirk on 23rd May 1962.

A near sister, the *Ben-my-Chree*, was delivered from the same builders only four years later,

Dover *(Nick Robins)*

by which time the overall cost of building had risen to £1.4 million. The two ships were converted from two-class to single class in 1967.

Two diesel ferries were built to the same basic design: the *Mona's Queen* in 1972 and the *Lady of Mann* in 1976. These ships came from the Ailsa Shipbuilding Company at Troon, and construction costs had risen to £2.1 million for the first ship and an inflationary £3.8 million only four years later. They did have slightly different machinery, the *Mona's Queen* being equipped with two 10 cylinder PC2 Crossley Pielstick engines, whereas the *Lady of Mann* was given about 15% more power with two 12 cylinder engines from the same manufacturer. The ships could carry 1600 passengers and nearly 100 cars, but accommodation for freight vehicles remained limited to light vans with a maximum weight of 3 tonnes and a maximum height of 2.2 metres.

The value of the four ships is demonstrated by the amount of traffic they encouraged onto their owner's services. During 1961, only 10,500 cars and 15,000 motorcycles were shipped. By 1967, with the two steamers in service, the numbers had risen to 34,500 cars and 31,000 motorcycles, and by 1978, two years after the last of the quartet had come into service, the annual figures had risen to 78,000 cars and 60,000 motorcycles. The significance of the motorbikes is, of course, the annual TT Races, but numbers have declined greatly in recent years.

The four ships served their owners well, despite direct competition from the Manx Line with the stern loading *Manx Viking* which operated between Heysham and Douglas between 1978 and 1987. The Manx Line was taken over by Sealink in 1984 making the element of competition even more intensive. Rising fuel costs eventually put paid to the two steamers, the *Manx Maid* being broken up on the Mersey in 1986 and the *Ben-my-Chree* suffering the same fate three years later in Spain. The *Mona's Queen* was laid up on a care and maintenance basis after the 1990 season. The *Lady of Mann* remained in service for the start of the 1995 season alongside the stern-loading vehicle and passenger ferry *King Orry*, formally the French flag train ferry *Saint Eloi*, but operated as the *Channel Entente* in 1989 (see Chapter 2). The *Lady of Mann* was then chartered out to a Portuguese operator for the summer.

Not all the first generation ferries and their associated routes were successful. The decision by the Ellerman's Wilson Line to augment their unit-load cargo services and modest passenger capacity, traditionally maintained by the fleet of so called "green parrots", to a fully fledged vehicle and passenger ferry service between Hull and Gothenburg, could not have been taken lightly. The stern-loading ferry *Spero* was completed by Cammell Laird in 1966. Described in the press as the most elegantly appointed ferry on the North Sea, she had luxury accommodation with 408 passenger berths, ample garage space for car and freight vehicles, and strangely, just like the Belfast boats, a hold forward designed to accommodate standard containers.

With the arrival of the *Spero*, the cargo steamers *Cicero* and *Rollo*, which could carry 12 passengers, were displaced, with both ships finding temporary solace on their owners Mediterranean services. The *Spero* was a big ferry for the day, she had a gross tonnage of 6916 and was 138 metres long and 21 metres broad. As an overnight and a day ship (the journey was scheduled to take 36 hours), her service speed was a modest 18 knots, but the *Spero* is probably the most unsung heroine of the embryonic car and vehicle ferry story of the 1960s. She boasted

Eagle *(Nick Robins)*

two spacious public rooms, each with its own bar and one with a dance floor, a restaurant, a self-service cafeteria, a teenage room complete with juke box, shops and of course, a Swedish-style sauna.

She entered a trade for which she was not entirely suited. She was slowly diverted towards reliance on the mini-cruise market in order to sell her passenger space (round trip fares started from £20 in 1969), only to find that she could not compete on the freight side with other container traffic to Scandinavia. Inevitably the service terminated in March 1972, the victim of being too much ahead of her time.

Transferred to a new service between Hull and Zeebrugge, the *Spero* championed a thrice weekly service which, ironically, was only laying the foundations for North Sea Ferries to follow. In April 1973, at the age of only 7, her career on the North Sea ended and she became the *Sappfo* under the Greek flag.

The demise of the *Spero* was brought about in anticipation of the transfer of two of the most innovative first generation ferries, the *Norwave* and the Dutch-flag *Norwind*, to the new North Sea Ferries service between Hull and Zeebrugge. The announcement that the two ships were to switch to the service was made in November 1972; the transfer being completed in 1974 following the arrival of the *Norland* and the *Norstar* (see Chapter 15) which took over the Europoort service. North Sea Ferries had originally inaugurated the Hull to Zeebrugge link on 20th November 1972, using the chartered German stern loading freighter *Norcape*.

The *Norwave* had originally opened the new Hull to Europoort overnight service on 17th December 1965, in direct competition with the Associated Humber Lines unit-load and passenger service between the same ports. The latter company's ships, the *Melrose Abbey* and

Bolton Abbey, had survived the one-sided competition only until the end of 1971.

The *Norwave* had a gross tonnage of 4038, a length of 110 metres and a breadth of nearly 18 metres. Both the *Norwave* and the *Norwind* were built by A G Weser at Bremerhaven. They were single screw ships and were driven by a type V314D Smit-Bolnes engine which gave them a service speed of 15 knots.

They were-drive through ships, bow loading at Hull and stern loading at Europoort and Zeebrugge. They had two vehicle decks each with a headroom of 4.1 metres which provided for 200 cars or a combination such as 60 cars and 65 lorries or trailers. There were sleeping berths for 187 passengers, and a further 48 passengers could be accommodated in couchettes and reclining seats. There was always a bowl of fresh fruit in each cabin before departure.

The public rooms were on "B" Deck; a large lounge and bar at the forward end, reception area amidships, and the cafeteria aft. There were a few "special" cabins on "B" Deck which were separated from the public rooms by sound-proof bulkheads. The remainder of the cabin accommodation was beneath the lower vehicle deck.

By comparison, the newer *Norland* and *Norstar*, were designed with a passenger complement of 1200, and vehicle accommodation for up to 135 twelve metre freight trailers or 252 cars.

On the English Channel, another new company, Normandy Ferries, was created to operate first generation vehicle and passenger ships. Two ships were completed for the company by a consortium comprising Ateliers et Chantiers de Bretagne and Dubigeon-Normandie at Nantes in 1967; they were the *Dragon* registered in Southampton and the *Leopard,* registered at Le Havre. The new service between these same two ports commenced with the *Dragon* on 29th June 1967. She was joined by her French sister in May 1968. A twice daily service was operated

***Blenheim** (Nick Robins)*

with simultaneous departures at 1130 and 2230, the day sailing taking 7 hours, whereas the overnight journey was scheduled to take over 8 hours.

With the first arrival of the *Dragon* at Southampton, several open days were held. The passenger accommodation was certainly second to none; in addition to the day accommodation, there were 500 berths, her total passenger capacity being 850. She had an uncluttered main garage and a small open freight deck aft, the latter partly reclaimed by additional cabin accommodation during the 1968/69 refits. At that time the size of her main garage was akin to an aircraft hanger; she had space for 260 cars or 60 trailers.

The basic Le Havre service was supplemented by a summer only Le Havre to Rosslare service which ceased in 1971. Occasional off-season cruises were operated to Rouen in the early days of the company. In due course, Normandy Ferries took delivery of the magnificent cruise ferry *Eagle* in 1971, another product of the Nantes yard. This ship had a gross tonnage of 11,609, and could accommodate 650 passengers. The *Eagle* opened a new service to Lisbon on 18th May and to Tangier on 22nd May. In 1972 she was joined by the *SF Panther*, formerly the Travemunde-Trelleborg Lines *Peter Pan* and dating from 1963. Her maiden voyage for Normandy Ferries was to Le Havre on 20th November 1972.

The fortunes of the southern Europe services fluctuated with the seasons and the two ships struggled to break even. A plan to extend the route of the *Eagle* to include the Canaries in 1975 was curtailed with her sudden withdrawal and sale to French owners. The *SF Panther* was also withdrawn and later became the first vehicle ferry on the former Coast Lines Seaway route between Aberdeen and Lerwick as the *St Clair* (Chapter 13).

Meanwhile the *Dragon* and *Leopard* persisted on the Le Havre service. The UK terminal transferred to Portsmouth in December 1984. However, during the following month, the company, which by then was part of the P&O Group, was sold to Townsend Thoresen and the

St George *(Nick Robins)*

Horsa *(Miles Cowsill)*

ships were integrated into that fleet. The *Dragon* finished at Portsmouth in 1986, and following a short refit, during which she received an old Atlantic Steam Navigation Company name, the *Ionic Ferry*, commenced between Cairnryan and Larne on 10th July 1986. There she carved a popular niche for herself, until she was eventually withdrawn in 1992.

Other first generation car and passenger ferries include the Townsend Free Enterprise fleet (Chapter 7); strangely also the magnificent 9200 tons gross *Blenheim* built for Fred Olsen Lines in 1970, but registered in London, the latter became Scandinavia World Cruises *Scandinavia Sea* in 1981. In addition there were a number of popular and well known British Rail ferries including the *St George* and the *St Edmund* at Harwich, the *Hengist* and *Horsa* at Folkestone, the *Senlac* at Newhaven, and the *Ailsa Princess* and *Antrim Princess* at Stranraer, plus those vessels already described in Chapter 6.

The *St George* and the *St Edmund* were built in 1968 and 1974 respectively and maintained the Harwich to Hoek van Holland service at 21 knots (daytime). The *St George* could accommodate 1200 passengers and 220 cars (210 lane-metres) and the *St Edmund* 1400 passengers and 290 cars (387 lane-metres). The *St George* eventually went to Cypriot owners in 1984, becoming the Florida based *Scandinavia Sky II* in 1990, whereas the *St Edmund* had been sold the previous year to the Ministry of Defence to become HMS *Keren*, a transport vessel used in the Falkland Islands War. She later became Cenargo's *Scirocco*, and is fondly remembered as the Channel Island Ferries *Rozel* starting in the 1988 season. She now operates between Morocco and Spain.

The three sisters *Hengist*, *Horsa* (latterly the *Stena Hengist* and *Stena Horsa*) and the *Senlac* were completed in 1972/3 and could carry 1400 passengers and 217 cars (366 lane-metres). The *Senlac* carried the distinctive funnel colours of the Newhaven-Dieppe joint service with SNCF and passed into complete French ownership in 1985. The *Hengist* and *Horsa* were designed for the Folkestone to Boulogne route and were sold for further service in the Mediterranean when that service was terminated in 1992.

The *Antrim Princess* and the *Ailsa Princess* were completed for the Stranraer to Larne service in 1967 and 1971 with room for 1200 passengers and 155 and 200 cars respectively. They were popular ships, the *Ailsa Princess*, being characterised by distinctive Italian styling. The *Antrim Princess* was chartered to the Isle of Man Steam Packet Company in 1986 as the *Tynwald*, and was sold on to Italian owners in 1990 as the *Lauro Express*. The *Ailsa Princess* became the *Earl Harold* in 1985, when she adopted mainly relief duties including a freight only service to Boulogne. She was sold in 1989 to Greek owners.

THE NEW INTERNATIONAL COMPANIES

North Sea Ferries and Normandy Ferries were the first examples of international cooperation in the development of short sea vehicle and passenger traffic. Both of the new consortia included the General Steam Navigation Company as a major driving force. Both ventures were, and are, in their hybrid form, highly successful.

North Sea Ferries was created by a consortium of two German, two Dutch and two British companies: respectively the Argo Line and Kirstens'; the Holland Steamship Company and Phs. van Ommeren; and the General Steam Navigation Company and Tyne Tees Shipping. Agreement had been reached by the consortium on operational details and the design of two vehicle and passenger ferries to operate between Hull and Europort as early as June 1964.

The subsequent withdrawal of Kirstens' and the take over of Coast Lines (Tyne Tees Shipping) by P&O (the parent of the General Steam Navigation Company) soon gave P&O a share of more than a third in the new company. Modern day operation of the company sees it as a 50/50 joint venture with the Royal Nedlloyd Group, with a fleet of ten ships.

The General Steam Navigation Company was also instrumental in the creation of Normandy Ferries. This new company was an Anglo-French venture promoted by Southern Ferries, which, to all intents and purposes was the General Steam Navigation Company, and the Société Anonyme de Gerance et d'Armement (SAGA).

The General Steam Navigation Company had gained cross-Channel experience with the *Royal Daffodil* which ran from the Thames to Calais with a connecting overland "package" to Barcelona in 1965. Traditional "no passport" day trips to Calais and Boulogne had been operated over a number of years by the *Royal Daffodil* and the smaller *Queen of the Channel*, and in 1966 also by the *Royal Sovereign* (see Chapter 8) which ran cruises from Great Yarmouth to Calais. Expertise so gained was invaluable in the creation of the new company.

Normandy Ferries expanded into the prestigious Dover to Boulogne market using second hand tonnage and in January 1985 the company sold out to European Ferries Group (Townsend Thoresen) for a total sum of £12.5 million. The final irony in the Normandy Ferries story came in December 1986, with the announcement that the P&O Group had bought European Ferries Group for £450 million to form the formidable ferry giant we know today.

CHAPTER 10

FREIGHT FERRIES

The British freight ferry owes a great deal to its military heritage described in Chapter 5. The first purpose built freight ferries were the *Bardic Ferry* and *Ionic Ferry*, fine successors to the Landing Ships Tank, and built to the order of the Atlantic Steam Navigation Company in 1957 and 1958 respectively (Table 6). No other carriers were able to grasp the potential importance of roll-on roll-off freight traffic at that time.

It is important to recall that although the volume of Continental freight was far less in the 1950s than it is today, the number of operators, ships and routes was extremely diverse. Typical Continental traders were the Associated Humber Lines and the Ellerman's Wilson Line out of the Humber, the Bristol Steam Navigation Company out of South Wales, the British & Continental Steamship Company loading out of Belfast, Glasgow, Liverpool and Manchester for Amsterdam, Rotterdam, Antwerp, Ghent, Dunkerque, Terneuzen and Antwerp, and the Currie Line trading out of Leith between the Baltic and the Mediterranean. The list could go on: the General Steam Navigation Company, George Gibson & Company, the Great Yarmouth Shipping Company - and so on through the alphabet.

Many of the traditional cargo ships were replaced by container ships or modified to accommodate containers. The first ever purpose built container ships were the *Container Venturer* and the *Container Enterprise*, built by British Railways for their Heysham to Belfast service in 1958. These novel ships could carry 65 B-type railway containers and were indeed the nucleus of the maritime container revolution which was to follow world-wide.

Many cargo ships were converted for the carriage of containers. Nevertheless, the dominant economics of wheeled freight soon overtook the container era, and a new breed of roll-on roll-off freight ferry soon started to compete on the market.

The new ferries were extremely successful, but not all the operators could raise the capital to progress, and others just did not have the right vision of the future and fell by the wayside. Many of the previously big-name operators disappeared in the evolutionary process, others promoted consortia, whose origins are now no longer recognisable, with the sole aim of raising sufficient cash to invest in the new and expensive technology. Relentlessly, the traditional cargo ships were lined up at the breakers yards, with the relatively new container ships, slightly more defiant in their resilience, following all too soon.

What of the ships themselves; how did the concept of the *Bardic Ferry* progress to the giant proportions of the *Norbay* and the new *European Seaway*-class? Was the progression merely one of ever increasing size? To a certain extent economy of scale did drive the development of the freight ferry, but engineering advances in all fields have had an equal influence in design.

The progression is summarized in Table 6. It shows that there has been a surprisingly small number of freight ferries built into the British register, the majority of the ships have been bought-in second hand, particularly from Scandinavian companies. Secondly, the pioneering of the Atlantic Steam Navigation Company in designing and building the *Bardic Ferry* and her running mates is strikingly shown at the head of Table 6.

The third point that the Table shows is the gradual increase in size of the freight ferry through the 1960s and 1970s. These were the two decades when expansion and new routes led to an almost insatiable appetite for more ships. The 1980s was a decade of consolidation with no new building. But in the 1990s the freight ferry returned anew in the form of the super-ferries of the *European Seaway*-class and the *Norbay.*

The *Bardic Ferry*-class each had a main vehicle deck which was accessed via a stern loading door. The headroom on the vehicle deck was 4.4 metres, ample for the commercial vehicles of the day. There was room for 70 lorries or trailers. The upper deck was designed for containers, but was later modified for the carriage of vehicles with the removal of the 20 tonne crane. The ships, although designed as freight carriers, were also provided with excellent two-class accommodation for 55 passengers. The *Bardic Ferry* commenced service between Preston and Larne on 2nd September 1957 and the *Ionic Ferry* followed her into service on 10th October 1958.

The next pair were the *Cerdic Ferry* and the *Doric Ferry.* Essentially similar to the two earlier ships, their passenger complement was smaller with cabin accommodation for only 35. Two 16-cylinder Paxman turbo-charged oil engines gave the ships a service speed of 14 knots. Although all four ships were built with bow rudders, bow thrust units were later also installed.

The next ship was the *Gaelic Ferry.* She was launched from Swan Hunter and Wigham Richardson's yard on the Tyne on 3rd October 1963. Her service speed was 16 knots, and she was powered by two 2-stroke single acting 10-cylinder Sulzer engines. Her original passenger accommodation was only for 28, but this was increased to 44 in 1972. In the following year her freight capacity was increased when the ship was lengthened by 23 metres to give her an overall length of 134 metres.

The last ship to be built by the Atlantic Steam Navigation Company was the *Europic Ferry.*

Bardic Ferry *(Ferry Publications Library)*

***Cerdic Ferry** (Ferry Publications Library)*

She entered service between Felixstowe and Europoort on 18th January 1968. She required a crew of 52 and had accommodation for 44 passengers. She was driven at 18 knots by two SEMT Linholmen-Pielstick oil engines, which enabled her to make the crossing in just under 6 hours. In addition to the main vehicle deck and the upper deck there was a small lower vehicle deck abaft the engine room which was used mainly for export cars. She could carry 62 twelve metre trailer units or 272 cars. A survivor of the Falkland Islands War, she was ignominiously renamed the *European Freighter* in 1992 before being sold out of the fleet.

In the early days each vessel had one master who was responsible for his ship. For example, Captain Hockings, although one-time master of both the *Bardic Ferry* and the *Ionic Ferry*, was sent to Tilbury in November 1967 to collect the *Doric Ferry* and bring her to Preston. This then became his ship. Similarly, Captain Close was master of the *Ionic Ferry* for the 13 years prior to the transfer from Preston to Cairnryan. Contrast this with the intense crewing schedule of the *Gaelic Ferry* when she was near the end of her career and operating as a freight-only ship out of Dover in 1988. At that time the ship had three crews working on a rota of 24 hours on, 48 hours off, but the manning level had gone down to a crew of 32.

The *Destro* and *Domino* are typical early freight ferries. They were built by Ankerlokken Verft A/S in Norway for the Ellerman's Wilson Line service between Hull and Gothenburg. These ships had a service speed of just over 17 knots provided by two 8-cylinder Linholmen-Pielstick engines driving controllable pitch propellers. They had room for 34 trailers on the main deck and a further 18 trailers on the shelter deck. Access to the main deck was by means of a stern ramp which was strong enough to withstand loads up to 70 tonnes, and to the shelter deck via a lift. All the freight ferries of this era were built with the dual purpose of carrying containers rather than trailers in anticipation of container traffic outstripping wheeled traffic.

Puma *(Nick Robins)*

This was not to happen.

Following the collapse of the short-lived Sealord Shipping Company of Great Yarmouth (Chapter 11) the Norfolk Line progressed from a long standing unit load service to roll-on roll-off with the introduction of the *Duke of Holland* on their service to Scheveningen on 28th January 1969. With a capacity of 758 tons gross, she could carry 24 trailers and had special accommodation for up to 60 cattle. She was joined in 1972 by the *Duke of Norfolk* which offered a slightly larger gross tonnage of 948. Norfolk Line was taken over by Maersk Line in 1973, who introduced a Chatham to Zeebrugge service with the *Duke of Anglia*. The company also inaugurated Middlesbrough, Esbjerg and Scheveningen services before finally out-growing Great Yarmouth in favour of Felixstowe as its southern base.

An important class of freighter is the Townsend Thoresen *European Gateway* class. The first three ships (the *European Gateway*, *European Trader* and *European Clearway*) were built by Schichau Unterweser AG (SUAG) of Bremerhaven to a standard design. They offered 1000 lane-metres of space for trailers, plus room for up to 32 export cars; there are 52 cabin berths although the passenger certificate is now for 132. The fourth ship, the *European Enterprise* was built in 1978; she was renamed *European Endeavour* in 1988. The *European Gateway* was lengthened by 16 metres in 1980 and her passenger certificate was enlarged to 326. In this capacity she was transferred to Larne to run alongside the *Free Enterprise IV* (see also Chapter 14).

Variations on freighter design continued throughout the 1970s. The pause in new-building throughout the 1980s heralded a totally new concept of freight ferry: the *European Seaway*-class, built by Schichau Seebeckwerft AG in Bremerhaven. P&O European Ferries planned four new ferries as part of a £200 million development of the Dover to Zeebrugge service; in the event the fourth ship was actually completed as the passenger ship *Pride of Burgundy*. The first of the freighters entered service on 7th October 1992.

The *European Seaway* and her sisters are 179 metres long, and 28 metres moulded breadth. They have a gross tonnage of 22,986 and have a service speed of 21 knots produced by four Sulzer 8-cylinder ZA type four stroke oil engines. Each pair of engines is coupled through a reduction gearbox to a Lips controllable pitch propeller made of stainless steel. There are no bow rudders, but rather two Lips controllable 20 tonne bow thrust units. The ships also feature an anti-heeling system, two retractable fin stabilizers and a bulbous bow.

There are two vehicle decks, each bow and stern loading, through doors which are 8.5 metres wide by 5 metres high. The Main Deck offers a total capacity of 975 lane-metres and the Upper Vehicle Deck a further 950 lane-metres. This enables the carriage of 120 fifteen metre long accompanied vehicles, equivalent to a cargo deadweight of 4600 tonnes on a draught of 6 metres. Accommodation is provided for 200 drivers in 43 two-berth cabins and 38 two-bed cabins fitted with an additional Pullman berth. The crew complement is 50. The standard of accommodation is very high reflecting the expectations of lorry drivers today as well as an element of competition from the Channel Tunnel.

The new ships comply with the International Maritime Organisation stability requirements (1990) for a two compartment standard of damage stability. They also have full fire protection and sprinkler systems in the passenger accommodation, with a drencher system fitted in the vehicle decks and foam monitors in the dangerous cargo areas.

The new *Norbay*, and her Dutch sister the *Norbank* are equally impressive. They were built

European Endeavour *(Miles Cowsill)*

Norbay *(Miles Cowsill)*

Stena Challenger *(Miles Cowsill)*

for North Sea Ferries Hull to Europoort service at a cost of £62 million at Van der Giessen-de-Nord shipyard in Rotterdam. The two ships have a service speed of 22 knots. They are powered by two 8-cylinder and two 9-cylinder Sulzer 7A 40S oil engines. These give them 20% more power than the passenger ships *Norsea* and *Norsun* (Chapter 15), and enable the freighters to cut the voyage time by 4 hours to only 10 hours, with one hour being lost with the new riverside berthing facility at Hull.

The *Norbay* and *Norbank* have a capacity of 18,300 tonnes gross, being some 167 metres long by 23 metres broad. They have three freight decks each with a free height of 4.9 metres, which offer a total capacity of 2040 lane-metres or about 150 trailers. Access to the freight decks is via a 9 metre wide stern ramp to the Main Deck level, and there is a fixed ramp up to the Tank Top. A hoistable ramp leads to the Upper Deck, which is limited to axle loads of up to 30 tonnes. The other two decks can take vehicle weights up to 45 tonnes. The ships have accommodation for 114 drivers in two berth cabins each with en suite facilities. They require a crew complement of 30, and all the crew occupy single cabin accommodation with en suite facilities. They entered service in the winter of 1993/94

P&O PANDORO FERRIES

Work on a new linkspan at Fleetwood was carried out during 1974 in anticipation of the start of a new service to Larne in April 1975. The operator was the newly created P&O Pandoro Ferries, then working in close liaison with the Belfast Steamship Company, which was also in the P&O Group.

Two new ships, the *Bison* and *Buffalo*, were built for the service by J J Sietas in Hamburg. The pair had a gross tonnage of 3484 tons. The stern ramps cope with loads up to 60 tonnes, and there is an internal 32 tonne lift between the main and lower deck.

In due course a new service was provided to Dublin. In 1979 two new purpose built ships, the *Puma* and the *Ibex*, were introduced at a cost of £18.5 million. The ships were especially designed for the Fleetwood to Dublin service. The British and Irish Line soon joined this new enterprise; the *Puma* was bareboat chartered to them, and was delivered in their colours with the name *Tipperary*. The ships are larger than the original pair, have a gross tonnage of 6310, and are 150 metres long by 22 metres broad.

The *Ibex* and *Tipperary* were built in Japan by Mitsui Zosen. Up to 125 12 metre trailers can be carried on the main tank top deck, main deck and upper deck, all of which continue under the deck house forward. Trailers are loaded via a 12 metre wide stern door onto the main deck. Access to the upper deck is via a fixed internal ramp and to the tank top deck via a 40 tonne lift. There is accommodation for 29 crew and 12 drivers.

The *Ibex* lasted just over a year on the new service before she was displaced by chartered tonnage. She was then transferred to North Sea Ferries where she became the *Norsea* (in 1980) but she was renamed *Norsky* in November 1986, returning to P&O Pandoro Ferries' Dublin to Liverpool service in 1995. The *Tipperary* eventually followed her sister to North Sea Ferries in 1989 to become the *Norcape*.

Second-hand replacement tonnage was found to fill the gap: the chartered *Union Melbourne*, built in 1975, became the *Puma* in 1980, and the *Viking Trader*, having led a nomadic existence under many flags since her building in 1976, and previously used by P&O European Ferries out of Portsmouth, joined the fleet vice the *Tipperary* in 1989.

In 1988 the Dublin service was transferred to Liverpool where new facilities were available within the Freeport complex. At that time the *Tipperary* and the *Buffalo* maintained this route, and the *Bison* and the *Puma* were kept on the Fleetwood to Larne route. With the departure of the *Tipperary* in the following year, both the *Bison* and the *Buffalo* were lengthened and their accommodation upgraded to give them a capacity of 1190 lane-metres or 90 freight units, and passenger accommodation for 60 drivers.

The *Bison* was painted in British and Irish colours but the *Buffalo* retained Pandoro blue, now the P&O dark blue with the house flag on the funnel. The two ships remained on the Liverpool to Dublin route until 1994 when the *Puma* replaced the *Bison*. The *Viking Trader* came onto the Fleetwood to Larne service to replace the *Bison* when she first moved to the Dublin service, but the *Viking Trader* now runs alongside the *Bison*, the latter returned to P&O Pandoro Ferries colours, and now with sponsons fitted amidships. Chartered tonnage has also been used on both services.

In January 1993 the P&O Belfast to Ardrossan service was transferred to Pandoro and based at Larne. The ship, the *Belard*, built in 1979 as the Danish *Mercandian Carrier II*, has a modest freight capacity of 410 lane-metres on the Main Deck and 374 on the Upper Deck, and she maintained one round trip per day: Belfast (or Larne) depart at 1800 hours, Ardrossan depart about 0300 hours the following morning. Rescheduling with the Fleetwood service allowed the ship to be withdrawn and sold to the Isle of Man Steam Packet company during the Autumn of 1993, but recently chartered back to her old route with P&O Pandoro Ferries.

At the other end of Ireland a new service between Rosslare and Cherbourg was started in November 1993 using the *European Clearway*, previously on the P&O European Ferries service between Dover and Zeebrugge. The ship can accommodate 46 trailers and has a passenger certificate for 107.

Replacement tonnage for the *Bison* and *Buffalo* is now on order. The new ships will carry up to 140 trailers and will have accommodation for 100 drivers. Their service speed will be 22 knots which will reduce the crossing time between Liverpool and Dublin to only six and a half hours as opposed to the current eight hours. New terminals are being built both at Dublin, and at Liverpool, where a riverside terminal is under construction avoiding the necessity to lock in and out of the dock system.

TABLE 6. PRINCIPAL FREIGHT FERRIES BUILT FOR THE UK REGISTER

Ship	Built	Gross Tons	Owner
Bardic Ferry	1957	2550	ASNC
Ionic Ferry	1958	2557	ASNC
Cerdic Ferry	1961	2455	ASNC
Doric Ferry	1962	2573	ASNC
Gaelic Ferry	1963	3316	ASNC
Europic Ferry	1967	4190	ASNC
Duke of Holland	1969	758	Norfolk Line
Tor Mercia	1969	1600	Tor Line
Tor Scandia	1969	1600	Tor Line
Destro	1970	1599	Ellerman's Wilson Line
Tor Belgia	1971	4130	Tor Line
Domino	1972	1582	Ellerman's Wilson Line
Duke of Norfolk	1972	948	Norfolk Line
Hero	1972	3375	Ellerman's Wilson Line
Tor Gothia	1972	4128	Tor Line
Baltic Enterprise	1973	4668	United Baltic Corporation
Baltic Progress	1974	4668	United Baltic Corporation
Bison	1975	3453	Pandoro Limited
Buffalo	1975	3453	Pandoro Limited
European Gateway	1975	3953	Townsend Thoresen
European Trader	1975	3353	Townsend Thoresen
European Clearway	1976	3335	Townsend Thoresen
Duke of Anglia	1977	2632	Norfolk Line
Elk	1977	5463	Poets Fleet (P&O)
European Enterprise	1978	3367	Townsend Thoresen
Baltic Eagle	1979	6376	United Baltic Corporation
Ibex	1979	6310	P&O
Puma (Tipperary)	1979	6310	P&O
European Seaway	1991	22986	P&O
European Highway	1992	22986	P&O
European Pathway	1992	22986	P&O
Norbay	1993	18000	North Sea Ferries

CHAPTER 11

CAR CARRIERS, HEAVY PLANT AND GENERAL CARGO

There were once three very beautiful Royal Mail Liners, "The Three Graces", which were named the *Amazon, Arlanza* and *Aragon.* They had been built in 1959 and 1960 by Harland & Wolff for the South American passenger service, and they had a large refrigerated capacity for frozen meet. At the age of only eight they matured into three equally fine Shaw Savill Liners, respectively the *Akaroa, Arawa* and *Aranda.* Within two years they were sold to Uglands and Leif Hoegh of Norway and turned into ugly slab-sided car carriers - gone was all the former elegance and grace. Such was the market for the carriage of export cars that the three car carriers traded, initially as the *Akarita, Hoegh Trotter* and *Hoegh Traveller* and later under a variety of other names, until withdrawn and scrapped in the early 1980's.

The Ocean Steam Ship Group, through their subsidiary Elder Dempster Lines, became involved with the export car trade in the North Sea in 1965 when they formed Seaway Car Transporters Limited. The first ship to be built for the company was the British designed stern- and side-loading car carrier *Carway,* which was built for them at Grangemouth. She was a small ship with a gross tonnage of only 866, but she incorporated three car decks which ran the full length of the ship, with a part-length lower deck forward of the engine room.

A similar but slightly larger ship, the *Speedway,* was built by Robb-Caledon at Leith in 1970. On delivery, her name was changed to the *Clearway.* The company also bought in two second hand vessels of similar design, the *Mandeville* and the *Sealord Challenger,* the latter

Aberthaw Fisher *(Nick Robins)*

built with sister *Sealord Contender* by the Sealord Shipping Company of Great Yarmouth for a short lived service to Holland and Scandinavia. These ships were given the names the *Skyway* and *Clearway* respectively. The *Clearway* confusingly became the *Speedway* at the same time that the *Speedway* became the *Clearway*. The *Clearway* (ex-*Speedway*) had her decks strengthened in July 1971 at South Shields to enable her to carry heavy commercial vehicles. Thereafter she traded between Poole and West Africa. Her final voyage was from Las Palmas to Poole in April 1978, after which she was sold to Irish ownership.

The Ugland Group has maintained a number of their smaller car carriers under British registry over the years. The car carriers are a familiar sight in many UK ports such as Goole and the Thames; they bear the familiar *Auto-* names and now carry the consortium title "UECC" on the funnel. The vessels come in a variety of shapes and sizes, but they are all high-sided with numerous low-headroom car decks, some of which are hinged. Like the Elder Dempster ships, they are all stern-loading but they also have the facility for simultaneous side-loading as well. Typically they are of 1000 to 2000 tons gross.

Two rather unique roll-on roll-off ships were built to the order of James Fisher in 1966 under a long term charter arrangement to the then Central Electricity Generating Board. The ships carried Fisher names and livery but had the Central Electricity Generating Board logo on their bridge fronts. The ships were the *Aberthaw Fisher*, built by the Ailsa Shipbuilding Company at Troon and named after a power station in South Wales, and the *Kingsnorth Fisher*, built by Hall Russell and Company at Aberdeen and named after a power station in the Medway area. The the two ships were used to move heavy plant and machinery from its manufacturer to coastal power generating sites, many of which did not have proper harbour facilities.

The two ships carried a large hinged roadway on the upper deck behind the accommodation block. This could be raised or lowered between goal posts forward, and raised and lowered hydraulically astern. In this way large and heavy wheeled loads could be driven on and off over the stern. The payload was anything up to an incredible 700 tonnes. Amidships was a large hold to which access was gained via a lift. Temporary mooring facilities were constructed in order that the ships could get into some of the sites, but the ships had, in any case, a surprisingly shallow draft of only 4 metres.

The *Aberthaw Fisher* and *Kingsnorth Fisher* were initially based out of Number 3 Pomona Dock at Manchester. The maiden commercial voyage of the *Aberthaw Fisher* was from Manchester to Barry; she carried a 225 tonne transformer, a 215 tonne stator core and its 120 tonne outer casing.

Mention must also be made of the little fleet of coastal ships operated by J & A Gardner & Company of Glasgow. These ships are conventional coasters save for a bow ramp which gives access for heavy wheeled loads onto the hatch covers. The ships were built by James W Cook at Wivenhoe. The main hold can accommodate bulk cargoes with a capacity of 700 tonnes, and the hatch covers are strengthened to take loads up to 175 tonnes. One of the ships, the *Saint Kentigern* was lost in bad weather off the Shetland Islands in November 1979; there was no loss of life. The current fleet comprises the *Saint Angus*, *Saint Brandon* and the *Saint Oran*.

CHAPTER 12

ESTUARINE AND SMALL ISLAND FERRIES

Although the Voith Schneider propeller had arrived in Britain in the late 1930s, its adoption was very much delayed by the Second World War, and the subsequent availability of materials and parts from its German manufacturer. Indeed, the Red Funnel ferry *Vecta* had her Voith Schneider units removed due to lack of spares immediately after the war; they were replaced with conventional screws and diesel-electric drive. The *Vecta* and her younger sister the *Balmoral* could carry 17 cars loaded over a side ramp.

During the war itself, three small barge-like craft were built by Swan Hunter & Wigham Richardson for the Ministry of War Transport in 1942. They were named the *Empire Chub*, *Empire Dace* and *Empire Roach*; they had bow-loading gates to their open foredecks and accommodation and engines three-quarters aft. They were small with a capacity of only 716 tons gross and were driven by triple expansion engines. The *Empire Dace* was lost at Missolonghi in Greece during December 1944, but the *Empire Chub* and *Empire Roach* were to survive in post-war years under the management of Townsend Bros. Car Ferries (Chapter 3) for whom they maintained the North Shields to South Shields ferry service until the new Tyne Tunnel took over in 1962.

One of the first post-war built Isle of Wight ferries, the *Farringford*, was built as a diesel-electric paddle ship even though her running mate was the Voith Schneider driven *Lymington*. All other ships built for the Isle of Wight services have used the new technology. Table 7 shows how the ferries developed in size and capacity; the Yarmouth to Lymington ferries limited by the restrictions of the Lymington River.

Freshwater *(Nick Robins)*

Carisbrooke Castle *(Nick Robins)*

Shipbuilding costs went through £0.3 million to build the *Cuthred*, to £1.8 million for the three *Caedmon*-class ships, to £7 million for the *St Faith*. Whilst the Red Funnel Group operating between Southampton and Cowes was acquired by Associated British Ports in 1989, the British Railways ferries passed into the ownership of Wightlink, part of the Sea Containers Group, but in 1995 Wightlink was sold to CINVen Limited. The two newest Isle of Wight ferries, the *Red Falcon* and the *Red Osprey* were built for £16 million, and a third ferry is on order.

The *St Catherine*-class brought a new dimension to Solent travel. The *St Catherine* has a crew of only 17, but her Class IV Certificate enables her to carry 1000 passengers in summer and 905 in winter. She can carry 88 cars on the main vehicle deck and another 54 on the mezzanine decks beneath the central accommodation. With the mezzanine decks raised, she can carry 24 commercial vehicles.

Despite the new propulsion system, four post-war paddle ferries were built. On the Forth crossing, traffic warranted two new ferries: the *Mary Queen of Scots* built by Denny in 1949 and the *Sir William Wallace* which came from Denny in 1956. Both ships had oil engines with hydraulic drive and chain coupling.

It is noteworthy that as far back as 1947 the Forth Road Bridge Order had been passed by Parliament. But the two new paddlers were only displaced by the bridge on its opening on 4th September 1964, some 19 years after the Order was approved. On the opening of the bridge, the Denny owned and operated ferries (Messrs Denny & Brothers having gone into liquidation in September 1963) had by Statute to be sold to the owners of the ferry passage, now British Railways. Of the four ferries in operation at that time, only the *Sir William Wallace* was to see further service, and that under the Dutch flag on the Ijsselmeer. Two years later, the three remaining Tay vehicle ferries, the *B L Nairn*, *Abercraig* and *Scotscraig* (Chapter 1), were withdrawn at the opening of another new bridge, the Tay Road Bridge, on 18th August 1966.

Nearly the very last passenger and vehicle ferry to be commissioned with paddle wheels was the *Cleddau Queen*. She was built by Hancock's Dry Dock Company at Pembroke Dock in 1956 for Pembokeshire County Council. This little ferry, which had a gross tonnage of only 158, was a steamer, with twin 2-cylinder compound diagonal engines which were oil fired. She had room for about eight cars loaded over the sponsons fore and aft of the deck housing. However, the Voith Schneider propeller caught up with the paddle only six years later when the new *Cleddau King* arrived on the scene. Experience with the new ship soon saw the steam paddler converted not only to diesel propulsion, but minus her paddles as well.

There was to be one more paddler, the *Dartmouth Higher Ferry*. She replaced the steamer of the same name on the Sandquay Point to Old Rock chain ferry. Built by her owners, Phillip & Sons, she is diesel electric with a passage speed of 5 knots.

Just as the Forth and Tay crossings were replaced by bridges, so too were many other crossings: the Southampton Floating Bridge, Erskine, Ballachulish, Kylestrome, Kessock (Inverness), even Hull to New Holland when the new Humber Bridge opened in June 1981. The construction of nearby road tunnels relegated some car ferry services to passenger only, for example the North to South Shields ferry and the Tilbury to Gravesend ferry.

There remains a variety of cross-river services, including the chain ferries between Sandbanks and Studland, Cowes to East Cowes, the *King Harry Ferry* across the River Fal, the *Reedham Ferry* across the River Yare, and the Torpoint Ferry. Double ended cross-river ferries are operated between Portaferry and Strangford across the entrance to Strangford Lough in Northern Ireland, Corran and Ardgour across Loch Linnhe, across the Clyde and elsewhere.

The Skye ferry was maintained for a long time by turntable ferries, each able to carry 4 cars. The turntable ferry first emerged in Scotland in the first part of the century as a motorised wooden barge

Cenred *(Nick Robins)*

***St Faith** (Miles Cowsill)*

with a turntable capable of carrying one car. Four turntable ferries were to be commissioned for the Skye crossing: the first was the *Portree* in 1951, then the *Broadford* and the *Lochalsh*, and finally the *Kyleakin* in 1960. On summer Saturdays in the late 1960s queues of 2 to 3 hours duration were not uncommon and drivers were forced to start and end family holidays at the most strange times of day in order to avoid the worst of the hold ups.

The little turntable ferries were finally replaced in 1970 and 1971 by the double ended ferries *Kyleakin* and *Lochalsh* (now the *Carrigaloe* and *Glenbrook* at Cobh, County Cork). These ships could carry up to 28 cars and were able to cope with all but the heaviest weekend traffic without delay. Twenty years later they two were replaced by the larger *Loch Dunvegan* and *Loch Fyne*, which carry 36 cars and 250 passengers. The new Skye Road Bridge now completed, this service too will disappear in 1995.

The new Skye ferries are a larger development of the *Isle of Cumbrae*, which is a double ended ferry originally commissioned in 1977 for the Largs to Cumbrae Slip service on the Clyde. She carries 15 cars and 160 passengers, but has now been displaced to the Lochaline to Mull service by the new *Loch*-class ferries *Loch Linnhe* and *Loch Striven.*

The "island"-class of small Caledonian MacBrayne ferry has been hugely successful in providing low capacity vehicle ferry services. The *Kilbrannan*, built in 1972, was the first of the class to enter service. These small bow-loading ships have accommodation for 6 cars and 50 passengers and are a common sight throughout the west coast of Scotland. They are currently being replaced by the new *Loch*-class, which are bow and stern loading and have a larger capacity for 12 cars and 203 passengers. The one exception is the *Loch Buie* which can carry 250 passengers, but fewer cars in order to fulfil her role on the Mull to Iona ferry which is very popular with day visitors to the Sacred Isle.

Competition to the Caledonian MacBrayne car ferry service between Gourock and Dunoon is

Fylga *(Nick Robins)*

provided by Western Ferries (Clyde). They have operated a variety of second hand tonnage on the service since 1973, including the *Sound of Sanda*, formerly the old Southern Railway ferry *Lymington* (see Chapter 1), and the *Sound of Seil*, formerly also an Isle of Wight ferry, the *Freshwater*. The *Sound of Sanda* was finally withdrawn from service at the grand old age of 53, a remarkable achievement for any ferry, let alone one of Britain's first Voith Schneider propelled roll-on roll-off car ferries. The present fleet of four double ended ships each carry between 25 and 30 cars. The Caledonian-MacBrayne service is maintained by two ships out of the *Juno*, *Jupiter*, *Saturn* and *Pioneer*, the others are used for charter work and the Rothesay service. They can carry 40 cars and over 650 passengers.

Western Ferries (Argyll), an associate of Western Ferries (Clyde) until 1985, introduced the *Sound of Gigha* to the inter-island Feolin to Port Askaig service in 1969. She had been built as a bow-loading freighter for the carriage of lorries on a charter basis in 1966 for Eilean Sea Service with the name *Isle of Gigha*. As the Isla to Jura ferry she carries up to 28 passengers and 8 cars. Since 1974 the Scottish Transport Group (see Chapter 13) discontinued calls at Jura and so the little ferry now has a secure existence.

Development of inter-island ferry services in the Shetland Islands was hastened with the strategic involvement of the islands in the North Sea oil boom. Inter-island services were maintained by the North Company's conventional passenger and cargo ship, the *Earl of Zetland* until her retirement at the end of 1974 when the responsibility passed to Shetland Islands Council. In that year the *Grima* entered service, the first of three identical sisters each with bow visa and stern door. They are capable of carrying 10 cars and 93 passengers.

On arrival at each unmanned terminal a crew member leans forward to pick up the control box for the shore linkspan and adjusts it for the tide before unloading can begin. A second hand ferry was acquired from Norway in 1980 and retained both her Norwegian name, the *Kjella*, and the goal post derricks from her former existence. The Islands Council now maintains a comprehensive service on a

***Strangford Ferry** (Nick Robins)*

regular and reliable basis. Fares are heavily subsidised so as not to penalise residents on the smaller outlying islands.

The Orkney island services were maintained until very recently by the cargo ship *Islander* and the larger *Orcadia.* Again the services were taken over by the Islands Council, but the original company name of Orkney Islands Shipping Company was retained until recently when the company was retitled Orkney Ferries. The first car ferry was the *Lyrawa Bay* which operated the Scapa Flow services to Hoy and Flotta until displaced by the *Geira* from Shetland, later renamed the *Hoy Head.*

The first purpose built ship was the little bow loader *Eynhallow* She has a passenger certificate for 100 and can carry 8 cars or one lorry up to 80 tonnes. She is driven by twin Volvo Penta engines which give her a service speed of 10 knots. She commenced service between Tingwall (Mainland) and Rousay, Egilsay and Wyre on 24th August 1987. So successful was she in generating roll-on traffic to the islands that she was lengthened by 5 metres in 1991. A similar but larger ship, the *Shapinsay* was completed in 1989 and the even larger *Thorsvoe* followed in 1991, the latter built at a cost of £1.8 million with capacity for 96 passengers and 16 cars.

Pride and joy of the Orkney fleet are the twins *Earl Sigurd* and *Earl Thorfinn,* which bear traditional company names of former steamers. The twins entered service on the North Isles routes in 1990. They can carry 145 passengers and 26 cars. They were joined in 1991 by the *Varagen,* built in 1989 for the one time ill-fated Gills Bay to Burwick route in direct competition with the P&O Scottish Ferries' service between Scrabster and Stromness. Difficulty in engineering the terminals put paid to the proposal and the *Varagen* was taken over by the Island Council and put in service alongside the Earls after a protracted lay up at Grangemouth. She has the largest capacity of all, with room for 150 passengers and 40 cars.

VOITH SCHNEIDER PROPULSION

The Voith Schneider rotating-vane propeller was first successfully tried on the German State Railway ships on Lake Constance in the mid-1930s. The device comprises a series of vertically mounted vanes, perhaps a metre or a metre and a half in length by up 0.3 metres wide. The vanes have a cross section similar to the wing of an airplane.

The vanes are mounted below a disc assembly attached to the bottom of the ship's hull, and they are rotated via servo motors driven by the main engine. The vanes can be turned by controls on the ship's bridge in order to vary the direction of thrust from forward to reverse or to any other direction around the compass.

The units are commonly mounted in pairs or threes. The old *Lymington* had two units at diagonally opposing corners of the ship. The *St Catherine*-class have three units, one forward and two at the stern. The propellers dispense with the need for a rudder and for bow thrust units. The manoeuvrability offered by the Voith Schneider propeller allows accurate and easy handling of vessels in confined waters without the need for tugs or harbour lines. The system has been universally adopted for all the smaller ferries which have short crossings and many berthing operations to carry out during the course of a working day.

TABLE 7. ISLE OF WIGHT FERRIES BUILT SINCE THE SECOND WORLD WAR

Name	Built	Gross tons	Passengers	Cars
Farringford	1947	489	812	36
Carisbrooke Castle	1959	672	900	45
Freshwater	1959	363	620	26
Camber Queen	1961	293	165	34
Fishbourne	1961	293	165	34
Osborne Castle	1962	736	900	50
Cowes Castle	1965	912*	866*	67*
Norris Castle	1968	922*	866*	65*
Cuthred	1969	704	400	80
Caedmon	1973	761	750	70
Cenred	1973	761	750	70
Cenwulf	1973	761	750	70
Netley Castle	1974	1184	786	85+
St Catherine	1983	2036	1000	142
St Helen	1983	2983	1000	142
St Cecilia	1987	2968	1000	142
St Faith	1990	2968	1000	142
Red Falcon	1994	2881	700	140
Red Osprey	1994	2881	700	140
Red Eagle	1996		700	140

* After lengthening, winter 1975/76.

+ After modifications in 1980 to increase car capacity.

CHAPTER 13

THE LARGER FERRIES OF THE SCOTTISH ISLANDS

The Caledonian Steam Packet Company was formed in 1889 when the Caledonian Railway Company obtained powers to run steamers. It became part of the London, Midland and Scottish Railway Company in 1923, and came under nationalised railway ownership in 1948. David MacBrayne Limited was jointly owned by Coast Lines and the Transport Holding Company, originally also in association with the London, Midland and Scottish Railway Company. Coast Lines sold their 50% stake in 1969 when ownership passed to the newly formed Scottish Transport Group. Caledonian MacBrayne Limited was the product of David MacBrayne Limited and the Caledonian Steam Packet Company when they amalgamated in 1972.

Back in 1939 the London, Midland & Scottish Railway Company planned to build a dedicated car ferry with a capacity for 27 cars for service on the Clyde. The intervention of the war upset this plan and it was not until late in 1952 that an order was placed with Denny of Dumbarton. The result was the *Arran*; launched in September 1953, she inaugurated the Gourock to Dunoon car ferry service in January 1954 (see Table 8). The *Arran* was actually designed with the Ardrossan to Brodick service in mind, but a regular car ferry to Arran did not commence for some years; the new ship was in any case an instant success at Gourock.

Two sisters followed the *Arran* off the stocks, this time from the Ailsa yard at Troon; the *Cowal*, which joined the Dunoon service in April 1954, and the *Bute* which followed later in the year and opened the car and cargo service between Wemyss Bay and Rothesay. This second new route allowed the direct Glasgow to Rothesay cargo service to cease.

The three "ABC" ferries were of modest capacity. They were some 56 metres long by 11 metres broad, but they could carry 26 cars and 650 passengers. The passenger accommodation was on two decks. Immediately aft of the superstructure was a side loading hoist for the cars, and the car deck was aft of the hoist. They were driven by British Polar diesels and could maintain a service speed of just over 15 knots.

The after part of the car deck was reserved for cargo, usually in small containers, and these were loaded via the ship's own derricks. This facility was removed from all three ships in 1959, when the hold was plated over to enlarge the car deck and the samson posts removed. The ships were able to carry 35 cars. The *Arran* was eventually converted to stern-loading in 1972 for use on the West Loch Tarbert to Islay route.

The success of the "ABC" ferries promoted the order of a larger version of the same design. The order was placed in March 1956, for a ship which would cost £0.5 million, again from the Ailsa yard. Launched as the *Glen Sannox* on 30th April 1957, she made her maiden voyage to Brodick on 29th June, six days ahead of the planned date.

The *Glen Sannox* was a much bigger ship than her three forebears, with accommodation for 1100 passengers and 50 cars. She was 78 metres long with a broad beam of 14 metres. Her Sulzer engines could drive her at 18 knots. She was the first British passenger ship in which inflatable rafts were carried as part of the official life saving apparatus. The rafts replaced the buoyant seats and tanks which would otherwise have been carried and allowed the ship to trade with only two lifeboats.

In due course the side loading hoists on the *Glen Sannox* were complemented by a stern-loading ramp. The ship was finally sold out of service in 1989. Nevertheless the same principle, using side-loading hoists, was adopted by David MacBrayne Limited for the Western Isles services. Three new car ferries were built to the order of the Secretary of State for Scotland under the Highlands and Islands Shipping Services Act of 1960, for charter to MacBraynes.

The ships were built by Hall Russell & Company at Aberdeen at a cost of about £1.5 million. The three ships, the *Hebrides*, *Clansman* and *Columba*, respectively entered service on 15th April, 5th June and 30th July 1964, each bearing Leith as their port of registry rather than MacBrayne's normal home port of Glasgow. They had a summer passenger certificate for 600, with sleeping berths for 51. On the upper deck there was a lounge bar, the bureau, shop and cafeteria; on the promenade deck there was a large lounge and an open area aft.

Strangely, all three ships were equipped with an outside water dowsing spray system designed to wash away radioactive fallout in the event of a nuclear war. The design of the ferries was such that they would all have been commandeered for military use in the event of hostilities.

The three ships were driven by twin Crossley type HRP 8/47 turbo charged diesels and had a service speed of 14 knots. Cars, cargo and livestock were all loaded via the hoist which had a maximum capacity of 24 tonnes; about 52 cars could be carried. There were two turntables on the hoist and a third one at the far end of the car deck to facilitate vehicle handling. Headroom on the car deck was 3.4 metres, but reduced to 2.6 metres over the engine room where the deck was slightly raised. A water tight bulkhead separated the hoist well from the car deck at sea.

The *Hebrides* maintained the Uig-Tarbert-Lochmaddy triangle, the *Clansman* operated on the Armadale to Mallaig service in summer and deputised elsewhere in winter, and the *Columba* maintained the Oban to Craignure service. In the winter of 1972/73 the *Clansman* was lengthened by 11 metres and converted to drive-through operations. She maintained the Ullapool to Stornaway link for two years before moving to the Brodick service in 1976. She was sold in 1984. The *Columba* was sold in 1988 to Hebridean Island Cruises and converted for her new role as luxury cruise ship around the Western Isles where she now trades as the *Hebridean Princess*. The *Hebrides* was sold for service between Torquay and the Channel Islands in 1986, and renamed *Devoniun*. She was resold overseas in 1993.

The only serious competition in the Western Isles came from Western Ferries Limited in 1968. That year they opened a new terminal at Kennacraig towards the seaward end of West Loch Tarbert; the MacBrayne jetty was 5 kilometres further up towards the head of the loch.

The brand new *Sound of Islay* commenced running from the new terminal to Port Askaig on 8th April 1968 - a huge success, she was replaced by the larger *Sound of Jura* whose maiden voyage was on 27th July 1969. The *Sound of Jura* cost £0.3 million to build, was drive-through and included many other features never before seen in the Western Isles including children's play pens and a mother and children's room. Displaced from the new

Arran *(Nick Robins)*

Pioneer *(Nick Robins)*

Claymore *(Nick Robins)*

service, the *Sound of Islay* was put on a seasonal Campbeltown to Red Bay (County Antrim) service. She returned to the Islay service when the *Sound of Jura* had to be sold in 1976.

Western Ferries never received any Government subsidy. Nevertheless they carried the majority of the traffic to Islay from 1969 to 1975. The Monopolies Commission reported as follows in 1983, after the withdrawal of the service in 1981:

"By 1973 Western Ferries had established itself as by far the largest carrier of cars and commercial vehicles on the (Islay) route. David MacBrayne's belief that it could operate a profitable service was conditioned by unreasonable optimism about the rate of growth of revenue and the extent to which costs could be reduced.

The second crucial factor was the decision by the Secretary of State in 1975 to increase the subsidy given to the Scottish Transport Group's ferry services and not relate it to operating results on individual routes. David MacBrayne was able to offer a level of services to passengers, including car passengers which could not be matched by Western Ferries. If David MacBrayne had been required to break even or make a profit on the route we do not believe the company could have continued to operate the service. Because the granting of subsidy gave David MacBrayne the ability to follow a long-term policy we believe that Western Ferries, under financial pressure, took the decisions to sell the Sound of Jura, and to sell the lease of the pier at Kennacraig. This hastened the process of the withdrawal of the (Western Ferries) service in 1981."

The MacBrayne response had been to bring the *Arran* round from the Clyde in 1970 to offer a competitive hoist-loaded car ferry, instead of the passenger only service previously operated by the ageing *Lochiel.* The service was upgraded to stern-loading in 1972. In the mean time a purpose built ferry, the *Iona*, had been completed in 1970 in anticipation of a new terminal being constructed lower down the loch (towards Kennacraig). This was not to happen, and it was only when Caledonian MacBrayne acquired access to the Western Ferries terminal that the new ship could finally take up the service for which she was designed.

The *Iona* was built at the Ailsa shipyard at Troon as a side- and stern-loading ship. Her side hoist proved invaluable because she was able to operate a variety of services before moving to Islay. She carried a rather silly looking false funnel in her early days but this was removed in due course when her twin uptakes were adorned in the company colours.

Unable to get up to the old West Loch Tarbert pier, another smaller ship was built to take over the service to Port Ellen from the *Arran*. This was the stern-loader *Pioneer*, converted later in life to side-hoist loading as well, so that she could operate the Armadale to Mallaig service. She is a distinctive looking ship with her open car deck aft. The *Pioneer* undertook her maiden voyage to Islay on 14th August 1974. Access to the Kennacraig terminal was obtained in 1979 when the *Iona* finally took over.

In 1970 the *Glen Sannox* was displaced from the Brodick service by the *Caledonia*, with her much larger vehicle capacity, although her passenger complement was smaller. The *Caledonia* was built in Norway as the stern-loading car ferry *Stena Baltica* for the Stena Line, and she entered service between Gothenburg and Fredrikshavn on 25th April 1966. At the age of four she arrived in Scotland where she stayed until sold to Italian owners in 1988.

The next ship to enter the Caledonian MacBrayne fleet was the stern-loader *Suilven* in 1974. She had been ordered by A/S Alpha, a Norwegian company, for their Oslofjiord service from Moss at the end of the railway line out of Oslo. She was to have had the name

Isle of Arran (Nick Robins)

Bastø VI, but bought off the stocks, she was launched as the *Suilven* and put into service on the new Ullapool to Stornaway service displacing the *Iona*.

The *Claymore* was purpose-built. As a stern- and side-hoist loading ship she was an enlarged version of the *Pioneer*. On delivery from Leith in 1978 she took up the Oban Outer Isles, Coll and Tiree services.

The successor to the *Claymore* on this same route is the *Lord of the Isles*. She again is a revision of the basic *Pioneer* type of design, much enlarged and improved and with vastly superior accommodation to the *Claymore*.

Four more conventional looking ferries have also been built recently. They are the *Isle of Arran*, for the Arran crossing; the *Hebridean Isles* for the Uig triangle; the *Isle of Mull* for the Mull crossing, launched from the Ferguson Ailsa yard at Port Glasgow on 8th December 1987; the largest ever, the *Caledonian Isles*, which made her maiden voyage on 25th August 1993 when she replaced the *Isle of Arran* at Ardrossan; and the new *Isle of Lewis* now on station at Ullapool. The *Hebridean Isles* and the *Caledonian Isles* are the only major units in the fleet ever to be built out of Scotland, the former at Selby and the latter by Richards (Shipbuilders) Limited at Lowestoft.

Within her first year of service, the *Hebridean Isles* had 60 tonnes of ballast installed in her stern to improve her handling. Worse still, the *Isle of Mull* suffered serious deadweight problems when new, and for her first season in operation was unable to carry anything like her design load. She was sent to Middlesbrough in the Autumn of 1988 where an extra 5.4 metre section was added to her just forward of the funnel, in order to rectify the situation.

The *Hebridean Isles* has a gross tonnage of 5221, and is 94 metres long by 16 metres moulded breadth. She has a service speed of 15 knots and is powered by two Mirrlees Blackstone 8MB 275 oil engines, each connected to a controllable pitch propeller. She has twin Becker flap rudders, and two Brunvoll bow thrust units, plus rectractable fin stabilizers made by Brown Brothers. She is staffed by a crew of 30. The passenger accommodation includes an observation lounge below the bridge, a children's play area and a kiosk, with two cafeterias and two lounges, one of which has a bar. There is also a passenger lift.

THE 'NORTH' COMPANY

The only car ferry to be purpose built for the North Company (now P&O Scottish Ferries) was the *St Ola*, built at a cost of £1.4 million by Hall Russell and Company at Aberdeen in 1974. She was designed for, and operated all her UK career on the Scrabster to Stromness crossing of the Pentland Firth. She replaced the conventional passenger and cargo ferry of the same name.

She had a gross tonnage of 1344 and was 70 metres long by 15 metres broad. She could carry 400 passengers and 85 cars, although commercial vehicles were usually a major component of her payload, and up to 80 cattle or 320 sheep could be carried, again at the expense of the number of cars.

She was an excellent sea boat, as she needed to be trading across one of the most exposed coastal seaways in Europe. Occasionally, particularly in severe westerly weather, she took the sheltered, but slightly longer route through Scapa Flow.

The first car ferry on the Aberdeen to Lerwick route was the *St Clair* (ex-*SF Panther*, and originally built as the Travemunde Trelleborg Linnie's *Peter Pan*, see Chapter 9). This *St Clair* inaugurated the overnight Aberdeen to Lerwick car ferry service on 4th April 1977. She was only five years younger than the classic ferry of the same name which she replaced, demonstrating the rate at which ferry design was advancing, and the leading role that the Northern European designers and operators were taking in the development of the car ferry.

She was replaced in March 1992 by the fifth *St Clair*; built for the Gedser Travemunde Ruten in 1971. Formerly the *Tregastel*, of Brittany Ferries, and before that Yugoslavian-owned, the *Njegos* she can carry 600 passengers and 350 cars.

The *St Sunniva* joined the company to reintroduce the Aberdeen to Stromness and Lerwick service in 1987. She was formerly the *NF Panther* of Southern Ferries and was originally built as the *Djursland* in 1971 for Danish owners. She can carry 407 passengers and 220 cars.

The new *St Ola* has a capacity of 2967 gross tons and was built as the *Svea Scarlett* for the Stockholms Rederi AB Svea, of Sweden in 1971. She is older than the ship she replaced, but is much more spacious and can carry 500 passengers and 180 cars.

TABLE 8. MAJOR CLYDE AND WESTERN ISLES CAR FERRIES (AS BUILT)

Name	Built	Gross tons	Number of passengers	Number of cars
Arran	1953	568	650	26
Bute	1954	570	650	26
Cowal	1954	569	650	26
Glen Sannox	1957	1107	1100	50
Clansman	1964	2104	600	52
Columba	1964	2104	600	52
Hebrides	1964	2104	600	52
Caledonia	1966	1156	630	90
*Sound of Islay**	1968	280	93	20
*Sound of Jura**	1969	600	200	40
Iona	1970	1324	554	47
Juno	1974	854	674	40
Jupiter	1974	849	658	40
Pioneer	1974	1071	356	30
Suilven	1974	1908	408	120
Claymore	1978	1631	500	47
Saturn	1978	851	694	40
Isle of Arran	1984	3296	800	80
Hebridean Isles	1985	3040	500	80
Isle of Mull	1988	4719	1000	80
Lord of the Isles	1989	3200	1000	60
Caledonian Isles	1993	5221	1000	132
Isle of Lewis	1995	5000	1000	130

* Western Ferries Limited. The remainder of the ships were built for or acquired by Caledonian MacBrayne or their predecessors.

CHAPTER 14

SECOND GENERATION CAR FERRIES AND A NEW ERA

Although a number of second hand ships were coming into the UK registry, principally from North European owners, five major new units were delivered in the latter part of the 1970s. Four of these were for Townsend Thoresen and one for Sealink. The four Townsend Thoresen ships were the Super Vikings, of which the first, the *Viking Venturer* took up service between Southampton and Le Havre on 22nd January 1975. All four were built by Aalborg Vaerft A/S at Aalborg in Denmark.

The second Super Viking, the *Viking Valiant*, commenced her career on the Felixstowe to Zeebrugge service in May 1975. She transfered to the Southampton to Le Havre route for which she was built, only when the third ship arrived from Denmark. This was the *Viking Voyager*, which commenced at Felixstowe on 20th January 1976, and she was followed in May by the fourth and final ship, the *Viking Viscount.*

The ships, as delivered, have a gross tonnage of 6387 and are 129 metres long by 20 metres breadth. They are driven by twin Werkspoor TM410 8-cylinder and one central TM410 9-cylinder engines which gives them a service speed of between 18 and 19 knots. They originally carried 1200 passengers and 275 cars.

The fifth new unit of the late 1970s was also built at Aalborg, at a cost of £19 million. She was the *St Columba*, now renamed *Stena Hibernia*, and designed for the Holyhead to Dun Laoghaire route of Sealink. Her maiden commercial voyage took place on 27th April 1977 under the command of Captain Leonard Evans. The *St Columba* is larger than the Super Vikings, with a gross tonnage of 7836, she too is 129 metres long but is one metre wider at 21 metres breadth. She can carry 1700 passengers and 310 cars, and can maintain a service speed of over 19 knots.

The *St Columba* was used as the basic design for a quartet of ships built by Harland & Wolff for Sealink between 1979 and 1981 at a total cost of £64 million. They have almost the same dimensions as the *St Columba.* The first of them was the *Galloway Princess* which commenced service on the Stranraer to Larne service on 1st May 1980; she was followed by the *St Anselm* which was designed for the Dover to Calais route. The *St Anselm* arrived at Dover from Belfast under the command of Sealink's senior Master, Captain John Arthur. Her maiden voyage was undertaken on 27th October 1980.

The main difference between the new ships and the *St Columba* is that the new quartet have a drive-through upper vehicle deck and they also have twin funnels on either side of the ship which provide for uncluttered vehicle decks. The *St Anselm* had a passenger capacity of 1000, can carry 310 cars, and originally had a crew of 69. The *St Christopher* joined the *St Anselm* at Dover in March 1981, followed in June by the *St David* which was intended for use in the Irish Sea, but moved to a new Dover to Ostend service in 1985, and then to Stranraer in 1986. The French ferries *Cote d'Azur* and *Champs Elysees* (the latter chartered to Stena Sealink in 1992 for the Newhaven to Dieppe service as the *Stena Parisien*) were built as running mates to the *St Anselm* and *St Christopher* for the Dover to Calais service.

Functional and modern though the four ships are, they are by no means innovative. The

St Anselm *(Ferry Publications Library)*

St David *(Miles Cowsill)*

Stena Galloway *(Miles Cowsill)*

conservative state-owned company had clearly prescribed a traditional design within its contract specification. The *St Anselm* and the *St Christopher* were eventually displaced from the Dover station in 1990 by the West Indian registered *Stena Fantasia* and the French *Fiesta*; the latter ships have a capacity for 1800 passengers and 630 cars.

The prize for the innovative design of the early 1980s goes to private enterprise. In response to the Sealink move to concentrate on Calais (previously the Townsend port) rather than Boulogne (which was traditionally the railway port for the car ferries) with the *St Anselm* and the *St Christopher*, Townsend Thoresen placed an order for three new ships with Schichau Unterweser AG at Bremerhaven. The first of these was the *Spirit of Free Enterprise*, which was launched sideways into the water on 21st July 1979; her maiden voyage to Calais was on 14th January 1980. The next launch was the *Herald of Free Enterprise* on 21st December 1979, followed by the *Pride of Free Enterprise* on 31st May 1980.

As built, the ships have a gross tonnage of 7950, a length of 133 metres and a breadth of 23 metres. Of unconventional design their technical performance, with a service speed of 23 to 24 knots on triple screws, is most impressive; the power is provided by three Sulzer 2V/48 engines. The ships have two drive-through vehicle decks and with twin funnels set apart; both vehicle decks are entirely clear of obstruction. Amongst many innovations built into the new ships are the "Neat Stow" bow doors, forming a blunt and vertical prow which hinges outwards into two giant doors. The eight lifeboats are slung low within the superstructure, adding to the unusual appearance of the ships. Accommodation is provided for 1300 passengers on four decks; 350 cars can be carried.

Spirit of Free Enterprise (FotoFlite)

In January 1987 the *Herald of Free Enterprise* was covering for refits on the Zeebrugge service, with a view to modifications being undertaken for her to support this service on a permanent basis. On Friday 6th March disaster struck the ship, a disaster which was to put Europe in mourning, and a disaster which was to have far reaching ramifications for the future operation of vehicle ferries.

The ship was just 10 minutes out of Zeebrugge, having sailed with her bow doors inadvertently left open, and her bows still ballasted down to meet the Zeebrugge linkspan at high tide. At 12 knots the main vehicle deck began to take in water, and with only a few centimetres of water on the deck she listed over to port, regaining her posture just once before rolling completely over to port in a matter of just one minute. She sank in the shallow approaches to the harbour with two thirds of the ship submerged.

The ship was under the command of Captain David Lewry, one of her regular masters since 1980. She had 543 people aboard, of whom 193 perished - 155 passengers and 38 crew members. As the ship rolled over, the accommodation was immediately blacked out and the dark icy water of the North Sea rushed in through broken windows trapping people beneath glass partitions. The very thought of the conditions within that hull are horrendous.

In the subsequent Inquiry at Westminster, it was found that the design of the ship was blameless. The operation of the ship was, however, the subject of criticism, and with immediate effect, closed circuit television was installed on the surviving pair of sisters so that the bridge could view the integrity of the bow doors at all times.

We tend to think of the 'Herald' accident as unique. It was not. Only four years previously the *European Gateway* had foundered after a collision with the train ferry *Speedlink Vanguard* off Felixstowe on 19th December 1982. The crash caused a large gash in the hull allowing water to enter the ship below and then onto the vehicle deck. A sudden list of 45° occurred within three minutes of the impact, the stability of the ship was lost and she went over, again in shallow water. This time the roll took ten minutes to complete, allowing 64 of the 70 passengers and crew to be saved. There have been several other reported incidents around the world, the 'Herald' disaster with its massive loss of life was but the last straw.

A number of parliamentary instructions followed the 'Herald' disaster. The first was the provision of indicator lights and closed circuit television on the bridge to show the condition of all loading doors with effect from 1st January 1988. Independent supplementary emergency lighting became compulsory; passenger numbers had to be accurately monitored; bow and stern doors had to be closed at or immediately off the berth; draught gauges and loading computers should be installed; and so on. In addition, the British Government made funds available to research the stability of vehicle ferries in a damaged condition and this work allowed detailed representation to be made in due course to the International Maritime Organisation. This action was instrumental in precipitating that organisation's new damage stability requirements for one and two compartment ships published in 1990.

All passenger and vehicle ferries operating to the UK came under detailed scrutiny. Although all the ships were found to comply fully with the International Convention for the Safety of Life at Sea, a number of them were found, in due course, not to meet new damage stability requirements which were required in Britain ahead of the 1990 order of the International Maritime Organisation.

Modifications were possible on a number of ships, for example the little *St Ola* on the Pentland Firth had buoyancy sponsons built onto her hull and an anti-roll tank built above the bridge. There were several ships which had been built before 1980 that were not so easy to adapt. These included the *Earl Harold* (ex-*Ailsa Princess*) which was immediately flagged out to the Bahamas on charter to the British and Irish Line; the *Darnia*, which was withdrawn in 1991; the *Tynwald* (ex-*Antrim Princess*), and withdrawn in 1991; the *Earl Granville*, which was sold in 1990; and the *Pride of Canterbury* (ex-*Free Enterprise VIII*) and the *Pride of Hythe* (ex-*Free Enterprise V*) which were withdrawn at the start of 1993 (see Chapters 7 and 9).

A new era had begun. The new era was marked in a number of ways, not least in the renaming and repainting of most of the key players. This was the result of the sale of both Sealink to Stena Line in April 1990, and the sale of Townsend Thoresen to the P&O Group in December 1976, the latter at a cost of £450 million. The passenger ships of the Townsend Thoresen fleet were mostly given 'Pride' names, the *Spirit of Free Enterprise* was renamed *Pride of Kent* during 1987, and the *Pride of Free Enterprise* became the *Pride of Bruges* in 1988, the latter then attached to the Dover to Zeebrugge service.

The new Sealink Stena Line, now the Stena Sealink Line, systematically gave all their ships the prefix Stena. Amongst other name changes, the *Galloway Princess* became the *Stena Galloway*, the *St Anselm* became the *Stena Cambria* and was transferred to Holyhead, the *St Christopher* became the *Stena Antrim* for service at Stranraer, and the *St David* became the *Stena Caledonia* also at Stranraer.

CHAPTER 15

JUMBOISATION AND THE SUPER FERRY

During the 1980s, the economics of scale coupled with dramatically increasing demand, led to major alteration and enlargement of a number of existing ferries. Expensive though these operations undoubtedly were, they were certainly cheaper than building new ships. First to come under the surgeon's knife were the *Free Enterprise VI* and the *Free Enterprise VII* which were under pressure to satisfy increasing freight demand on the Dover to Zeebrugge route, and then the *Viking Valiant* and the *Viking Venturer* which needed greater capacity on the Portsmouth to Le Havre service.

Under a contract which amounted to £45 million, the four ships were each sent to Schichau Unterweser AG in Bremerhaven for alteration. The Zeebrugge pair were dealt with in 1985 and the Portsmouth ships during the winter of 1985/86. The work involved raising the superstructure and adding new fore-parts to each vessel. The superstructure unit of each of the Dover ships weighed some 1280 tonnes and was lifted off the hulls with four floating cranes. The new fore-parts were built together, back to back, and launched on 18th May 1985.

The two Free Enterprises each acquired an extra 16 metres in length. Their gross tonnage was increased to a massive 12,503, but their accommodation now provided for 1041 passengers and 330 cars as opposed to 1125 passengers and 220 cars before the metamorphoses. Ungainly though the ships now looked, they were spacious when compared with the two unchanged ships of the same class which then operated on the Dover to

Pride of Kent *(Ferry Publications Library)*

Boulogne route (*Free Enterprise V*, later *Pride of Hythe* and *Free Enterprise VIII*, later *Pride of Canterbury*).

In due course the *Free Enterprise VI* was renamed the *Pride of Sandwich* and the *Free Enterprise VII* became the *Pride of Walmer* (later the *Pride of Ailsa* and *Pride of Rathlin* on transfer to Cairnryan to Larne in 1992). While they remained on the Zeebrugge service they certainly kept their end up, running as they did with the more modern *Pride of Bruges* (ex-*Pride of Free Enterprise*) which was the third ship.

The superstructure of the two Super Vikings was too large to be lifted in one section and was dealt with in two parts. The same process was then carried out and a complete new vehicle deck was built before the superstructure was returned to the extended hulls. Both ships were back in service in time for the summer holiday period of 1986. In their new form they acquired a gross tonnage of 14,760, had become 144 metres in length and were now able to accommodate 1316 passengers and 380 cars or 60 freight units (cf 1200 passengers and 275 cars before conversion).

Under the renaming of the Townsend Thoresen fleet by P&O, the *Viking Valiant* became the *Pride of Le Havre* and later in 1994 the *Pride of Cherbourg*, whereas the *Viking Venturer* became the *Pride of Hampshire*.

The next ships to be elongated were the *Norland* and her Dutch-flag sister *Norstar*. The pair had been built in 1974 as second generation ferries for the Hull to Europoort overnight service of North Sea Ferries. They were themselves displaced from this route by new and larger tonnage (the *Norsea* and *Norsun* see below) in 1987. The opportunity was then taken to add an extra 20 metre long mid-section to the two ships. They returned to the Hull to

Pride of Kent *(FotoFlite)*

Free Enterprise VI (Ferry Publications Library)

Zeebrugge service, on which route they offer accommodation for 881 passengers and 500 cars.

The most recent passenger ferry to be put on the rack is the *Pride of Kent* (formerly the *Spirit of Free Enterprise*, see Chapter 14). She was sent to the Fincantieri yard at Palermo to receive major alterations which included the insertion of a new 31 metre section amidships, which increased her passenger capacity from 500 to 1825 and her car capacity from 350 to 460. The work cost a total of £20 million and took six months to complete. Her inaugural voyage as a "super ferry" took place between Dover and Calais on 17th June 1992.

Amongst the modifications that the *Pride of Kent* received were stability sponsons along the outside of the hull to comply with the International Maritime Organisation's damage stability regulations issued in 1990. She also features inflatable escape chutes and life rafts.

The *Pride of Calais* and the *Pride of Dover* are both products of Schichau Unterweser AG. They have a gross tonnage of 26,433 and are 170 metres long by 28 metres broad. They are driven by three CCM Sulzer A403 engines which give them a maximum speed of about 26 knots although their required service speed is 23 knots. They have accommodation for 2300 passengers and 650 cars. The first of the two ships, the *Pride of Dover*, was constructed in just 16 months. She undertook her maiden voyage between Dover and Calais on 2nd June 1987; the *Pride of Calais* followed her sister into service on 4th December 1988.

There has been only one British-built super ferry. The *Norsea* was launched by Govan Shipbuilders at Glasgow by Queen Elizabeth the Queen Mother on 9th September 1986. Built at a cost of £40 million, she was the largest passenger ship constructed on the Clyde

Norland *(Nick Robins)*

since the Cunard Liner *Queen Elizabeth 2*. She has a gross tonnage of 31,598, is 179 metres long overall, and 25 metres broad. Her four Wartsila Sulzer Type ZA 40 engines give her a service speed on her overnight passage of 19 knots, 3 knots slower than the new freighters *Norbay* and *Norbank*.

There are 268 two and four berth cabins which accommodate 746 passengers, and her total passenger certificate provides for a capacity of 1250. There were 2250 lane-metres of space on the vehicle decks; 137 twelve metre freight units and 232 cars could be carried, or with all the mezzanine decks raised a total of 850 cars. This capacity was reduced by 15 % in 1994 when buoyancy tanks were installed abaft the main vehicle decks to comply with the International Maritime Organisation's damage stability regulations introduced in 1990. The maiden voyage of the new ship took place from Hull to Europoort on 8th May 1987. Her identical, Japanese built and Dutch-flagged, partner the *Norsun*, entered service four days later.

A number of super ferries have been brought into the British registry. The first was the *St Nicholas* which operated the Harwich to Hoek van Holland service for Sealink. She flew the red ensign on her renaming from the *Prinsessan Birgitta* to the *St Nicholas* in June 1983 until she was flagged out in 1989. She is now the *Stena Normandy* operating between Southampton and Cherbourg, but still under a West Indian flag.

The *Stena Invicta* is another import. She was built in 1985 as the *Pedar Paars* for service between Kalundborg and Aarhus for the Danish State Railways. She was brought to Dover in July 1991 under her new name and registered at Dover. Her arrival boosted the Sealink Stena Line capacity on the Dover to Calais service during the competitive run up against P&O European Ferries to the opening of the Channel Tunnel in 1994. The *Stena Invicta*

Freight deck on the ***European Seaway*** *(Ferry Publications Library)*

Pride of Hampshire *(Miles Cowsill)*

Pride of Burgundy under construction *(Ferry Publications Library)*

Pride of Burgundy leaving Germany for her maiden voyage. *(Mike Louagie)*

carries up to 1750 passengers and 403 cars. The new *Stena Challenger* also arrived at her home port of Dover in 1991. She is primarily a freight carrier with 1500 lane-metres of vehicle space, but she can also accommodate up to 500 passengers. Other second hand super ferries are P&O European Ferries's the *Pride of Bilbao* (chartered from Irish Ferries), and the former Olau twins the *Pride of Le Havre* and *Pride of Portsmouth.*

The latest big ferry to be built for P&O is the *Pride of Burgundy*. Laid down at Schichau Seebeckwerft AG yard at Bremerhaven as the freighter *European Causeway*, plans were changed and she was launched on 16th May 1992 as a passenger and vehicle ferry to complement the super ferry fleet on the Dover to Calais service. The new ship has a gross tonnage of 28,138 and has accommodation for 1320 passengers and 600 cars. Her four Sulzer diesel engines give her a service speed of 21 knots.

Pride of Bilbao *(Ferry Publications Library)*

THE QUEST FOR SPEED

In the days of the steam turbine, when energy was cheap, there were a number of very fast cross-Channel day ferries. One of the earliest and fastest was the *Biarritz*, built for the Dover Strait service of the South Eastern & Chatham Railway Company in 1915 with a trials speed of 24 knots. The London and North Western Railway Company built the quartet *Anglia*, *Cambria*, *Hibernia* and *Scotia* in 1920/21 for the Holyhead to Kingstown (now Dun Laoghaire) service. The four ships had a service speed of 25 knots. The Southern Railway had the *Worthing* of 1928 running at 24 knots between Newhaven and Dieppe.

As energy costs increased, so service speeds dropped below the 20 knot mark. The dramatic rise in fuel costs that followed the Arab - Israeli conflict of 1973 finally put the turbine engine out of business and made operators look for reduced operation speeds for the motor ships. This trend continued until the arrival of the *Spirit of Free Enterprise* and her two sisters in 1980 and 1981; they had a handsome design speed of 23 knots and were actually capable of more. This increase of speed was the balance between the cost of speed, and the service required by the passengers, but it had only become possible with the advances in engine design and efficiency that had been achieved in the face of rising fuel costs.

An alternative form of fast sea transport was introduced to the Dover Strait with the arrival of car-carrying passenger hovercraft in 1968. These craft can maintain an incredible 60 knots and are quite resilient in adverse weather. They have a payload of 390 passengers and 55 cars. More recently they have been followed by the introduction of wave piercing catamarans: the Seacats operated by Hoverspeed, the *Condor 11* which operates to the Channel Islands and Stena Line's new services out of Holyhead and Fishguard. Most of these craft can carry over 400 passengers and 80 cars at 37 knots. Sadly none of them fly the red ensign.

These wave piercers are 75 metres long, slightly longer than a Jumbo Jet Airliner, but the next generation of fast catamaran will be 120 metres long. During 1993, Stena Sealink placed an order worth £128 million with Finnyards in Rauma for the first of a series of 40 knot catamarans. These will be able to carry 1500 passengers and 375 cars, or 50 lorries and just 100 cars. The craft will be powered by four gas turbine engines with water jet propulsion.

REFERENCES

Periodicals

British Ferry Scene (British & European Ferry Scene); Lloyd's Register of Shipping; Motor Ship; Paddle Wheels; Sea Breezes.

Books

Anon. 1976. *British Vessels Lost at Sea 1939-45.* (Cambridge: Patrick Stephens)

Chappell, C. 1980. *Island Lifeline.* (Prescot: T Stephenson & Sons)

Clegg, W P and Styring. 1962. *Steamers of British Railways and Associate Companies.* (Prescot: T Stephenson & Sons)

Coton, R H. 1971. *A Decline of the Paddle Steamer.* (Hull: Paddle Steamer Preservation Society)

Cowsill, M. 1990. *By Road Across the Sea, the History of Atlantic Steam Navigation Company Ltd.* (Kilgetty: Ferry Publications)

Cowsill, M and Hendy, J F. 1988. *The Townsend Thoresen Years.* (Kilgetty: Ferry Publications)

Duckworth, C L D and Langmuir, G E. 1956. *West Coast Steamers*, 2nd Edition. (Prescot: T Stephenson & Sons)

Duckworth, C L D and Langmuir, G E. 1967. *West Highland Steamers*, 3rd Edition. (Prescot: T Stephenson & Sons)

Duckworth, C L D and Langmuir, G E. 1977. *Clyde and Other Coastal Steamers*, 2nd Edition. (Prescot: T Stephenson & Sons)

Hendy, J F. 1985 *A Manx Enterprise* (Staplehurst, Kent)

Hendy, J F. 1989. *Sealink Isle of Wight*, (Staplehurst: Ferry Publications)

MacArthur, I C, McCrorie, I and MacHaffie, F G. 1965. *Steamers of the Clyde and Western Isles.* (Motherwell: Private)

McNeill, D B. 1969. *Irish Passenger Steamship Services, Volume 1, North of Ireland.* (Newton Abbot: David & Charles)

McNeill, D B. 1971. *Irish Passenger Steamship Services, Volume 2, South of Ireland.* (Newton Abbot: David & Charles)

Mitchell, W H and Sawyer, L A. 1965. *Empire Ships of World War II.* (Liverpool: Journal of Commerce and Shipping Telegraph)

Sahlsten, R, Söderberg, B and Bång, K. 1992. *Stena Line's Ships 1962 - 1992.* (Gothenburg: Stena Line AB)

Thornton, E C B. 1962. *South Coast Pleasure Steamers.* (Prescot: T Stephenson & Sons)

Thornton, E C B. 1972. *Thames Coast Pleasure Steamers.* (Prescot: T Stephenson & Sons)

Williamson, J. 1904. *Clyde Passenger Steamers from 1812 to 1901.* (Glasgow: MacLehose)

SHIP NAME INDEX

Names in ordinary typescript are roll-on roll-off vehicle ferries. Names in italics are passenger ferries, liners, cargo ships, ships of the Royal Navy, or other. The prefix HMS is given after the ship name, as in Halladale <HMS>. The year built is given in round brackets where known.

Hengist* and *Horsa (FotoFlite)

FERRY Publications

NORTH SEA FERRIES - ACROSS THREE DECADES 8.20
FERRIES OF PORTSMOUTH & THE SOLENT 8.20
BRITTANY FERRIES 1973-93 .... 8.20
FERRIES OF THE BRITISH ISLES 1995 .... 8.45
CAR FERRIES OF THE BRITISH ISLES 8.45
FISHGUARD – ROSSLARE 3.60
OLAU 4.10
INSIDE OLAU 13.50
WINSTON CHURCHILL 3.25
SAINT GERMAIN 3.25
EARL WILLIAM 3.25
SALLY LINE 3.50
FANTASIA 1.50
WIGHTLINK 4.10
P&O THE FLEET (3RD EDITION) 3.25
THE VIKING SAGA 4.50
HARWICH–HOOK (SOFTBACK) 9.85
HARWICH-HOOK (HARDBACK) 20.50
BY ROAD – ACROSS THE SEA 8.15
THE DOVER-OSTEND LINE 7.10
FERRIES OF DOVER 5.95
SEALINK STENA LINE 3.60
FOLKESTONE – BOULOGNE 3.60
THE HOVERSPEED STORY 4.10
KING ORRY 4.10
FERRIES OF THE ENGLISH CHANNEL 4.70
FERRIES OF SCOTLAND 5.70
STEAM PACKET MEMORIES 4.10
LIFE AND TIMES OF THE STEAM PACKET (SOFTBACK) 13.50
LIFE AND TIMES OF THE STEAM PACKET (HARDBACK) 20.50
FERRIES FROM PEMBROKESHIRE 4.10
CALEDONIAN MACBRAYNE - THE FLEET 4.70
PADDLE STEAMERS OF THE ALPS 5.30
NEWHAVEN-DIEPPE 4.70
FERRIES IN CAMERA 95 .... 8.45
FERRIES OF THE ISLE OF MAN - PAST & PRESENT 7.20
LADY OF MANN 3.80
FERRIES OF CORK 5.95

All prices are quoted to include postage and packing within the UK. For European and Overseas orders please add a further 85 pence per book and remit by Eurocheque or Sterling International Money Order or Giro cheque.

FERRY PUBLICATIONS, 12 MILLFIELDS CLOSE, PENTLEPOIR, KILGETTY, PEMBROKESHIRE, SA68 0SA.

Tel : 01834 813991 .... Fax: 01834 814484